EVERYTHING YOU NEED TO KNOW
ABOUT COLLEGE SPORTS RECRUITING

D0037139

Everything YOU NEED TO KNOW ABOUT COLLEGE SPORTS RECRUITING

A GUIDE FOR PLAYERS AND PARENTS

Jim Walsh with Richard Trubo

Foreword by Thomas Beckett,
Athletic Director, Yale University

Andrews and McMeel
A Universal Press Syndicate Company
Kansas City

Walsh, Jim, 1956–

Everything you need to know about college sports recruiting : a guide for players and parents / by Jim Walsh with Richard Trubo.

     p.   cm.

ISBN: 0-8362-2184-2 (pbk.)

1. High school athletes—Recruiting—United States. 2. Universities and colleges—United States—Admission—Planning. 3. College sports—United States. 4. College sports—United States—Directories. I. Trubo, Richard. II. Title

GV350.5.W35   1997

796.071'173—dc20   96-34773

                   CIP

This book is dedicated to my wife, Marie,
who not only heard my dream but saw it.
For the past eight years, she has loved, guided,
and inspired my efforts as a husband, father, and
businessman. She is a precious gift from God.

—J.W.

CONTENTS

ACKNOWLEDGMENTS

I would like to thank:

- God for directing my steps on a path that has led me into relationships and situations that have made me what I am today.
- My parents, Ken and Lorraine, and brothers, Dan, Tom, and Tim, who always encouraged me to pursue my dream.
- The parents, coaches, and, of course, the athletes whom I have been able to serve and guide—especially Ryan Lemmon, whose commitment and dedication serve as a legacy for others to strive for and surpass.
- My children—Kylee, Patrick, Melissa, Kimball, and Leah—who are in my thoughts each day.
- Tom Beckett, for bringing to this book his unique perspective on athletics and academics, and communicating the important role they play in college recruiting.
- All of my past coaches, teachers, teammates, and opponents.
- Richard Trubo, who demonstrated patience, humility, and the skills to translate my program into a book.

Finally, it is my sincere hope that all who read this book take away knowledge, insight, and guidance into their college recruiting experience that will help them reach their goals of studying and playing at—and graduating from—the college of their choice.

Jim Walsh

I gratefully acknowledge:

- Jim Walsh, whom I've watched nurture the lives of many student-athletes and help them prepare for meaningful futures.

ACKNOWLEDGMENTS

- Jane Dystel, our agent, who gave her usual total commitment and expertise to this book project.
- Matt Lombardi, of Andrews and McMeel, for his editorial guidance.
- My wife, Donna, from whom I continue to draw love and inspiration, day after day.
- My daughter, Melissa, who continues to impress me as she explores so many of life's great adventures.
- My son, Mike, whom I watch with pride as he approaches his college years and pursues his dreams.

Richard Trubo

FOREWORD

by Thomas Beckett
Athletic Director, Yale University

Each year, thousands of high school student-athletes dream of being recruited by coaches at America's colleges and universities. If you're one of the fortunate young men and women who is actively sought after, it is an experience that you and your family should cherish and enjoy. And if at the end of the rainbow, you gain admission to the college of your choice and are awarded an athletic scholarship as well, consider it a time for celebration.

But for too many student-athletes, the entire recruiting process is daunting and confusing. As young people meet and talk with coaches, the pressures and stresses seem to overshadow the excitement they should be feeling. Most of this anxiety, however, could be avoided if students and their families understood the process more fully, and clearly defined their own goals before the give-and-take between students and college coaches begins.

As you approach your own college years, the more information you have, the greater your chances of recruiting success. That's why I find this book by Jim Walsh such a valuable resource. "Product knowledge" is crucial in any field, and when you're "shopping" for a good education, a college degree, and a fulfilling athletic experience, you need to know how the system works and how you fit into it—which is precisely what this book will help you understand.

Let's not kid ourselves: Coaches are seeking the best athletes. At the same time, colleges and universities are looking for the best students. And if you've prepared yourself well both athletically and academically—establishing yourself as an attractive candidate to coaches and admissions offices alike—then you've placed yourself in control of your future.

Without doubt, you've spent hundreds and perhaps thousands of hours strengthening your body and refining your athletic skills. But, as Jim Walsh emphasizes in this book, you need to show just as much dedication in your pursuit of academic excellence. By succeeding both in the classroom and on the athletic field, you'll be in the unique situation of having a full range of opportunities available to you. Your options will include literally the entire list of colleges and universities in the country, and you'll find yourself in a great position to make decisions that are best for you.

My parents were educators, and my mother used to say, "The only commodity that America's young people are willing to be cheated out of is an education." If students were assured of a passing grade for a minimal effort, she said, most would settle for it. However, to become the best, you've got to invest—not only in building up your body but in nurturing your mind. That's some of the best advice you'll find in this book.

As your own recruiting process begins, be sure you already know what your own needs are and what you're looking for in a college and in an athletic program. Have you defined your academic major or area of interest? Are you interested in a public or a private institution? A large or a small school? A high-profile college or a lesser-known one? Might you be more comfortable in a Division I school, or perhaps one with a Division II or III ranking?

This book will help you understand the intricacies of recruiting that you'll encounter in the months (and perhaps years) ahead. College coaches frequently talk to high school students and their parents who are uninformed and even naive about recruiting. When student-athletes receive a letter from a coach, they assume that they're being aggressively recruited. But in many cases, while they may be on a list of prospects, the interest is only preliminary.

In much the same way, high school students might assume that a phone call, a home visit, or an invitation to travel to the campus is tantamount to a scholarship offer. However, that isn't necessarily true. Too often, young people and their families don't ask the key questions: "Where do I rank in your recruiting process? How badly do you want me to attend your college? Are you offering me a scholarship?" The more information that's out in the open and on the table, the better. If you don't ask questions and thus misread your situation, you could end up with little more than disappointment when signing day arrives.

You also need to make an effort to understand the National Collegiate Athletic Association's regulations governing student recruiting. These rules are designed to protect student-athletes, but they can be confusing, and they are not readily available to families who don't know how to access them (you can't go to a local bookstore and buy an NCAA manual). But you can read this book, which provides you with a road map along the college recruiting path that will help you understand the NCAA rules that guide this process.

So I believe there's a real need for Jim Walsh's book. When I was coaching at Stanford University and spent many hours a week recruiting, I would have appreciated having a book like this one to refer to students in order to answer their questions. It is an insider's look at college recruiting, and will help you make intelligent, well-informed choices. As Jim carefully explains, you *can* take control of your own recruiting, making certain that college coaches learn about your athletic and academic accomplishments, and what you'll be able to contribute to their program. This is an empowering guide that will help insure that your college experience will be a rewarding one. The time you spend reading this book will be a worthwhile investment in your future.

THE DREAM OF COLLEGE SPORTS

If you're among the six million boys and girls now playing high school sports, having the chance to compete at the next level—in college athletics—may be the dream of a lifetime. Perhaps while watching intercollegiate football or basketball on a Saturday afternoon you've imagined yourself on the field or the court, catching a touchdown pass or sinking a crucial free throw in front of a national TV audience. And you may have wondered how to get the attention of college coaches, earn a college scholarship, and give that dream a chance to come true.

For most high school students, however, the world of college sports is a mystery—complex, highly competitive, and seemingly impenetrable. The path toward playing at a college or university appears crowded and strewn with stumbling blocks. For many young people and their parents, uninformed about the intricacies of the recruitment process, this path becomes a minefield of anxiety, broken hearts, and shattered dreams.

I've seen many high school students with the physical, mental, and academic skills to play at the college level miss out on the chance because they didn't know how the college recruiting game is played. This book is intended to make sure you are equipped to take advantage of the opportunities in college sports that are out there for you. I'll describe how the recruiting process works from the perspective of colleges, what is required of you, and how you and your family can effectively manage your own recruiting to dramatically improve your chances of participating in athletics at the next level.

ARE COLLEGE ATHLETICS IN YOUR FUTURE?

At first glance, the recruiting process might appear weighted against you. After all, there are a limited number of slots on the athletic teams of America's colleges and universities, and millions of high school student-athletes are competing for them. To make matters worse, due to cost factors and the National Collegiate Athletic Association's changing limits on the number of available scholarships in particular sports, there are actually fewer athletic scholarships to go around now than in the recent past.

But as you will learn in these pages, you don't have to sit quietly by and leave your athletic and academic futures to the whims of fate. You will find out how to get your skills and talents evaluated fairly as a student and an athlete. Although your parents, coaches, teachers, counselors, and friends can assist you, it is really up to you whether or not *you* do what is required. It will take hard work, determination, and a keen focus on your goals. But whether you're a male or a female athlete, a high school senior or still several years away from entering college, you'll learn how to give yourself the best opportunity of getting the attention you deserve.

A PERSONAL PERSPECTIVE

I've been involved in sports at all levels—first as a four-sport letterman in high school, then as a college and professional athlete, followed by many years as a football coach and college recruiter. My coaching experience began at Yerba Buena High School in San Jose, California, during a strike-shortened National Football League season. My next coaching stints were at San Jose State University and Stanford University, where my recruiting responsibilities became national in nature. Since the late 1980s, I've operated A STEP BEYOND, a life management program for athletes, parents, and coaches designed to help young people develop athletically, academically, socially, and emotionally.

During all these years as a coach and a consultant, I've had access to hundreds of homes where many of America's finest young athletes have lived. And in those living rooms, I've heard so much confusion and so many misconceptions, that much of my time has been spent explaining the recruiting process and answering questions about how it works. Most students and parents are simply misinformed about many of the dos and don'ts of recruiting.

To further muddy the waters, many commercial "recruiting services" have emerged in recent years, offering to "market your son or daughter" by exposing these young athletes to hundreds or thousands of colleges. These services have created a newfound anxiety within the recruiting world—first, among parents who sign up and then nervously wait, still not knowing how the other side functions during the recruiting season; and second, among universities that are being inundated with letters about and videos promoting high school prospects . . . correspondence that has no business on the desks of some universities, and creates a work overload for college coaches. I suppose the scattershot technique succeeds from time to time. But I prefer to provide you with a plan that can make a direct hit for you *and* the college. Since the inception of my business in 1988, my goal has been to create a win-win scenario for both the athlete and the university, and in these pages, you'll learn how this can be done.

RECRUITING: EXHILARATING—OR DEMORALIZING?

As misunderstood as college recruiting is, the process really hasn't changed very much in the twenty-plus years of my involvement. Yes, the NCAA adopts new rules periodically, intended to eliminate questionable and even abusive activities of college recruiters. But for students and their parents, recruiting can still be a chaotic and demoralizing experience—except for those who have a road map to guide them over the potholes and around the quicksand that can leave young people discouraged and disappointed. For the athlete and his or her family, recruiting can still be an exciting and memorable experience—but only if it's well understood and managed skillfully.

Over the years, I've seen and heard of too many talented high school athletes who were misevaluated and disregarded too early in the process. At the opposite extreme, others were so inundated with attention that they became overwhelmed and were incapable of coping with it all. (Just imagine how you'd respond to personal phone calls from the head coaches of some of the nation's most prestigious universities!) Many of these young people "short-circuited" the process by assuming that the attention equalled an impending scholarship offer (which it often doesn't), and became lost in and victimized by the recruiting process.

Unfortunately, there's nothing scientific or always predictable about recruiting, and the competition for the limited number of scholarships can seem ruthless. There are many "roads" that present themselves to a candidate and his or her family, creating a maze of choices as jumbled as a Los Angeles freeway interchange. But there are proven strategies you and your family can adopt to move you toward your goal. In this book, you'll be guided along a direct path, taking into account every obstacle you'll encounter. I believe you can reach the goal that was once A STEP BEYOND your grasp—a goal *all* of my clients have achieved.

A COMMITMENT TO EXCELLENCE

Even to his own high school coach, Brian Luxemburger didn't appear to be a top college prospect. He was a linebacker on his high school football team in Orange County, California, and when I first watched him play as an eleventh grader, I saw natural talent that I believed would catch the eye of many college coaches. Brian had great defensive instincts, and he closed on the ball carrier in a manner indicating his willingness to hit with a vengeance.

After viewing a video of Brian in action, I told him that he looked as if he belonged in the media guide of one of our nation's service academies (Army, Navy, Air Force). Brian gave me an "Are you out of your mind?" look, and responded, "No way! I'm not that kind of guy!" But in less than two weeks, West Point had become Brian's first choice of a college!

Brian's high school coach, however, had not yet recognized what I already knew about this talented young athlete. But I strongly believed he could become a top recruit—if he became dedicated to making himself as appealing as possible to college coaches.

Our first goal was to take care of the factors Brian could control. Could he control his high school coach's opinion of him? No. Or the opinions of those who evaluated him? No. But could he control his grades? Yes. His work ethic? Yes. His off-season conditioning program designed specifically for his position? Yes. His total commitment to his team's winning a high school football championship? Yes. His capacity to lead by example? Yes. His willingness to discipline himself socially? Yes.

Brian, in fact, made the decision to spend Friday nights at his desk at home. He acknowledged that there are no academic quick fixes or gimmicks, and that to get good grades, he'd have to *earn* them. He learned some time-management skills, sought help from his teachers whenever necessary—and his efforts paid off.

Brian also began refining his physical skills, and even before spring practice he was in game-ready condition. While his weight increased fifteen pounds, his time in the forty-yard dash decreased by five-tenths of a second. His performance on the field and in the classroom caught the attention of everyone who came in contact with him.

We also assembled a six-minute videotape that demonstrated Brian's abilities as an inside linebacker. The video depicted not only his present abilities but also his natural talents, which college coaches could project into their own future plans.

In his senior season, Brian's football team won league and sectional titles. He was chosen captain, and earned the team's most valuable player award. He was voted all-league, all-county, and all-section. He improved his GPA (grade point average) to a level on a par with his athletic performance. Ultimately, his jersey was retired at his high school—and he received an athletic scholarship to Villanova University!

Brian had done it. Yes, he had plenty of support—from his parents, teammates, coaches, and my program. But here's the bottom line: It was Brian's body, his efforts, and his commitment that got him beyond the limitations he had once imposed upon himself.

Brian could have easily been one of those kids ignored and passed over in the recruiting process. But I was able to help him define his goals and create a realistic game plan for winning those shoulder pads on a college team.

A GUIDE FOR YOUR FUTURE

This book can help you reach your own goals, whether your dreams involve football, baseball, basketball, or any other college sport. Here is what you will find in the pages that follow:

- If you're a high school student—or the parent of one, or even a high school coach—you'll find out how recruiting is conducted from the college's point of view. You'll learn about the choreography of college recruiting—the dance between recruiter and student that can eventually win you a higher education and the opportunity to play college sports. Recruiting isn't something that begins when you're a senior, or is relegated to a particular time of the year. It's in perpetual motion, running year-round. Yes, there are timetables defining when coaches may contact recruits and when letters of intent can be signed. But the system never rests, and, in terms of your own preparation, neither should you. By following the guidelines in this book, you'll be able to go A STEP BEYOND so you do get noticed, and rise above the pack.

- You'll set goals, both immediate and long term. You'll define what *you* want to accomplish—not what your parents or your high school coach may want for you. These goals should cover areas from academics to athletics, and should come from your heart as well as your head. You'll also make a list of the colleges you'd like to attend, and then earmark the improvements in skill levels necessary to make yourself appealing to these institutions.

- You'll find assessment tools and "reality checks," designed to help you evaluate and improve your own "recruitability"—where you stand among your athletic peers, and areas where you may need to make more progress. You'll develop insights into your own drive, leadership qualities, mental toughness, self-confidence, and coachability. Your character is as important—and perhaps even more significant—than how far you can throw a football, how high you can jump at the volleyball net, or how impressive your performance records will be in the eyes of college coaches. You'll also get a sense of where you rank in terms of "cosmetic features"— height, weight, strength, and speed.

- You'll adopt a personalized training program designed to

take full advantage of your natural athletic gifts, one that takes into account the physical demands of high school and college sports. It will help you improve your vision, balance, power, flexibility, speed, and heart as they relate to sports and to everyday life.

- You'll develop an academic game plan, and make it *the* centerpiece of this program. If you don't have your studies in order, and if you haven't signed up to take the required college entrance exam (SAT or ACT), you won't be able to play sports at any level. Good grades will also win you instant attention from some colleges—the military academies and the Ivy League schools, for example—that *have* to pay attention to you if you've proven yourself on the playing field *and* in the classroom; they can only pursue those athletes who are also outstanding students, so if you've gotten your academic life in shape, you're out of the starting blocks a lot faster than most of your teammates.

  The students who have enrolled in A STEP BEYOND realize that although they can't change some of their physical attributes—such as how tall they are—they *can* control their grades. My young clients have earned a cumulative GPA of 3.5—and they have a 100 percent college placement record, due as much to their academic as to their athletic achievements.

- You'll be introduced to many young athletes with whom I have worked. The stories of their successes will become an inspiration as you strive toward your own dreams, academically and athletically. These students have survived and thrived through the recruiting process. While many (but certainly not all) of them are football players, their experiences contain lessons for athletes in every sport.

A "MUST-DO" ATTITUDE

So many of my student-athletes have developed motivational armor, equipped to deflect any negative or adverse situations they may encounter. This armor is "plated" with a "must-do" alloy, essential for accomplishing not only their athletic and academic goals but also to deal effectively with the demands and stresses that are part of college recruiting.

The right attitude can compensate for most personal shortcomings. You shouldn't feel held back by your natural size and strength; I have repeatedly seen hard work and heart overcome these kinds of apparent limitations. So many times, for example, I've watched athletes at small high schools, who you might think would not capture much attention from recruiters, yet who caught the eye of college coaches because they had made a commitment to excellence.

THE ART OF GETTING NOTICED

Bobby Masters didn't play high school football for a powerhouse program. In fact, his high school—St. Margaret's—fielded an eight-man football team. Many schools with eight-man teams and limited enrollments have a real sense of integrity in their sports programs, giving the kids a chance to play sports without worries about drawing huge crowds, booster-club pressures, or athletic-scholarship concerns.

But although Bobby was a talented and confident quarterback, he hadn't seriously considered what kind of commitment it would take to play at the collegiate level. Even so, he had many qualities that impressed me, beyond being able to throw the ball sixty-five yards downfield. He had speed, range, and courage. He put 110 percent into every play in every game, and was available wherever his coach needed him. One Friday afternoon, I saw him play not only quarterback but also linebacker, free safety, cornerback, tailback, and nose guard—all in the same game. Even though he had opportunities to transfer to other high schools with larger and more visible football programs, he remained loyal to his school and his teammates and decided to stay right where he belonged.

We put together a videotape of Bobby in action, containing a variety of plays showing his ability and versatility. Meanwhile, he worked hard to improve his throwing accuracy and his skills at tackling and running. And we made sure that college coaches knew that he fit into their academic profile by supplying an unofficial transcript.

Bobby did get noticed, and by some major university coaches. He was invited to visit Southern Methodist University in Dallas—the city where he was born. Three other schools were vying for his talents, too. Ultimately, Bobby accepted San Jose State University's offer of an athletic scholarship.

WHAT ABOUT YOUR PARENTS?

Remember, when you're looking ahead to playing college sports, you should be pursuing your own dreams, not those of your mom or dad. Sometimes, parents do become overly involved, pushing their children in one direction or another. Before long, the kids begin chasing a college scholarship for all the wrong reasons—and find themselves on the fast track toward an ulcer.

These are circumstances that you and your family *must* avoid. At the same time, however, your parents have a crucial role to play in your college pursuit, "managing" your overall efforts, in the best sense of that word. You are very precious to your mom and dad, and they can become your strongest advocates, helping you evaluate and get past the recruiter-babble and false promises that are often part of this process.

I advise your parents to participate in and oversee all your interactions with college coaches. They can bring balance and maturity to the table, where you might find yourself a little intimidated when talking to a bigger-than-life college coach who has shown up in your living room or has called your home. When you're talking to university representatives, it may be hard for you to say "no" or even ask the right questions. It's so easy to slip into a subservient role, but your parents can keep those conversations on a level playing field.

Meanwhile, throughout the recruiting experience, you need to remain vigilant, identifying areas where you might be falling short in the classroom, the training room, or on the playing field. Yes, you've taken an important first step by reading this book, but from this point onward, you and your family must take control of the recruiting process.

BECOMING THE BEST YOU CAN BE

There are few, if any, "perfect recruits." Everyone has qualities that coaches might consider weaknesses or "flaws." When I met Shawn Green, who is now an outfielder for the Toronto Blue Jays, he was sixteen years old and a member of the Tustin High School baseball team in California. Shawn was not yet fully physically developed (he weighed 162 pounds), but he had a beautiful, natural swing, and I thought he could become the next Don Mattingly. I remember telling Shawn's father that he would be a first-round selection in the baseball draft after his senior year.

However, I felt that Shawn needed to become stronger, although it was important not to throw just any weight-training program at him, since an inappropriate one could undermine his natural talents that obviously were already there. If he were placed on a workout regimen that did not take his own physical structure and natural growth cycle into account, it could impair his ability to run, throw, catch, and hit, and perhaps hurt his chances at ever playing college or professional baseball.

I worked with Shawn in drills to improve his speed, and he began a customized conditioning program designed to increase his size and strength. He shaved three-tenths of a second off his time in the 60 (a time measured by pro and college coaches). He also continued to excel academically, earning a 4.6 GPA on a 5.0 scale and scoring in the ninety-ninth percentile on a motivational inventory administered by major league baseball scouts as part of their evaluation of an athlete.

As Shawn prepared to graduate from high school, there was interest in him from many directions. Stanford University had already offered him a baseball scholarship, and at the same time, he was projected to be a first-round selection in the pro baseball draft. How could he lose? Although the situation seemed like a dream come true (and it was), Shawn had to battle the pressures of living up to a "star" billing. But he responded with maturity beyond his years (he was just seventeen). Selected by the Toronto Blue Jays in the first round of the draft, he signed a pro contract that guaranteed his education at Stanford, while awarding additional funds to the Stanford baseball program.

SET YOUR SIGHTS ON THE PRIZE

No matter what course you take in life, I want your adventure in athletics—in high school and college—to be enjoyable and rewarding. You may be in the enviable position of using your athletic talents as an avenue for helping pay for a college education, or at least helping you gain entrance to the college of your choice, even if you don't win an athletic scholarship. An advanced degree can become a springboard for achieving many of your lifetime goals.

Bear in mind that you are embarking on a race, with college entrance and perhaps a scholarship as the carrot that you and thousands of other young people are chasing. It can be an exciting and invigorating process, and if you follow the guidance in this book, it can be a thoroughly positive experience, too, beginning today and continuing until you finally earn a college diploma.

PART I

PUTTING YOUR BEST
FOOT FORWARD

CHAPTER 1

UNDERGOING A REALITY CHECK

Is there a college education—and college sports—in your future?

It's time to start the process that will help you answer that question. You need to evaluate your prospects for participating in college athletics realistically, and if the outlook appears promising, then you can place yourself on course to attract the interest of one or more colleges. This chapter will help you understand what your value to these schools is, and what you need to do to increase your worth, both academically and athletically, to these institutions. Although there are some personal characteristics you can't change, many others are well within your control, and thus you can direct this process to a greater degree than you may have once thought.

This chapter, then, will help you climb onto a predictable path to help you reach your goals. At the same time, however, there are no shortcuts to fulfilling your college dreams. You'll have to work hard—outthinking and outhustling most of the thousands of other students with the same aspirations. But college sports is an achievable goal if you get a sense of who you are today, and how to become a top prospect to whom college coaches will pay attention.

STARTING THE REALITY CHECK

Let's begin this self-evaluation. The first step is to honestly answer the question: "Do I really want to compete at the next level?"

Particularly since you're reading this book, you probably instinctively responded to this question with a resounding "Yes!" If you're like many high school athletes, you may have envisioned yourself playing college sports for years. But sometimes, these dreams are being pursued for all the wrong reasons.

Some students are brimming with athletic talent, and feel they should take advantage of it—even if their heart isn't in the game. Or perhaps those ambitions for competing in college really belong more to their parents than to themselves, and they just can't imagine disappointing mom and dad. If they're playing for their family and not themselves, however, they're going to be miserable at college.

So ask yourself the following questions:

- Why do I want to play college sports?
- Do I have a love of the game?
- Do I truly enjoy myself when I play my sport?
- Do I feel very much alive when I'm competing, and does that feeling affect other aspects of my life in a positive way? For example, have my grades gone up since I made a commitment to sports?
- Am I playing for my family members or for myself?
- Am I willing to put in the necessary time to compete at the next level?

Keep in mind that athletics at the college level require a huge commitment of both time and energy. The academic demands of college are enormous, and when you add sports to that equation, you need to have outstanding time-management skills and dedication to your studies when you're not on the practice field. The payoff, of course, can be enormous: a college degree that can give you a tremendous advantage in life, no matter how far you go in sports; and the rare experience of sharing a common goal in the intimacy of a team setting.

HOW DO YOU RATE ACADEMICALLY?

"I can throw the ball sixty yards, Jim. So what difference does it make if my grades aren't very good?"

I hear statements like this all the time. Many young athletes believe that the ability to shoot a jump shot or strike out batters is all they need for a ticket to the college of their choice. But without good grades, you may be watching games from the grandstands or on your TV set on Saturday afternoons.

In chapter 3, I'll discuss in detail how to get on the academic fast track. In the meantime, here are some of the most important questions to ask yourself in your reality check:

- What is my grade point average?
- What are my SAT scores?
- Is academics my number-one priority, and have I learned to balance my studies and sports so that I'm doing well in the classroom?
- On a daily basis, am I making sure my homework is done, that I'm well prepared for exams, and that I'm meeting regularly with my teachers for feedback on how to stay on course academically?
- Can I compete academically at the college level?

Face it: If you have a 3.2 GPA in a core course curriculum, you are a much more attractive candidate to many colleges than if your GPA is 2.5, 2.0—or less. To be eligible for sports, the NCAA has set a minimum standard of a 2.0 to 2.5 GPA (depending on your score on the SAT or ACT). But if you're able to show college coaches a 3.0 or 3.5 GPA instead, and perhaps 1,000 or more on the SATs, you've instantly put yourself in the upper echelons of the recruiting class. On the other hand, if your academic transcript reflects a 2.0 GPA, you're in a vast no-man's-land where your options are more limited, and where you won't get nearly as much attention unless your athletic skills are simply impossible to ignore.

TAKING ADVANTAGE OF THE POWER OF GOOD GRADES

Not long ago, I worked with a young football player named Tim Carey, who was one of the top five high school quarterbacks in the nation. Not surprisingly, he was a blue-chip recruit in the eyes of most college coaches in the country. But as a high school junior, Tim recognized that to open every conceivable door for himself, he needed to raise his grades a little. When I met him, his GPA was not commensurate with his goals. He had his heart set on attending Stanford University, but I explained that he would have to devote more effort to his academic life and study even harder—which he did, raising his GPA significantly. With the combination of his academic and athletic achievements, he could have gone to virtually any college. He chose Stanford, where he entered as a freshman in 1993.

(Because of coaching shakeups and other changes at Stanford, Tim transferred to the University of Hawaii in the fall of 1996. For more about Tim's transfer, see "When Circumstances Change" on p. 159—and note how he never lost sight of his academic goals.)

Throughout this book, you might be surprised that I'll keep coming back to your academic performance, and stressing its importance in the race for the college finish line. That's because scholastics are a factor within your control, and if you're excelling in the classroom, that will serve you well when colleges consider your overall profile, no matter what your athletic talents may be. If you want to put yourself on the recruiting map, make sure your academic life is in order. Yes, your ability to throw a football or run the 1,500 meters in a blur is important; but academic excellence can be the determining factor that separates you from others competing for "your" scholarship. If you can show recruiters an outstanding academic record in high school, many of them are going to think, "We can use someone like him in our program."

Remember, by qualifying on grades alone to get into a college—without taking your sport into account—you're really in a great position. But if your grades aren't yet up to par, what are you willing to start doing *now* in the classroom to promote your cause and make you a more attractive candidate? You need to exercise the same passion for your studies that you do for your sport.

HOW DO YOU RATE ATHLETICALLY?

As part of your self-evaluation, you need to take a close and honest look at your athletic abilities. Your answers to the following questions will provide information of interest to college coaches.

- What have my athletic achievements been in high school?
- How do my athletic skills and accomplishments compare to those of my high school teammates and players on teams we have played against?
- Have I been in the starting lineup of my high school team?
- Do I have statistics (e.g., running speed, size) that will catch the eye of college coaches?

- Does my body seem to respond well to the exertion of competition, and have I been able to rebound quickly from injuries?

- Have I received recognition by being named to all-star teams? Did I make all-league? All-county? All-state? Have I received any other athletic awards or honors (for example, "Player of the Week" recognition from the local newspaper)?

- How well did I fare at camps and tournaments? What kinds of evaluations did I receive at those camps?

- Do I have the physical skills to play at the college level? Are there college athletes whose abilities are similar to mine, thus helping me determine my own likelihood of succeeding at the college level?

- Do I know people currently competing at the next level whom I can use as a reference point, comparing my own talents to theirs and finding out from them what it takes to play in college? (Caution: Many people will tell you they played at the college level in the past, but somehow athletic prowess and achievements get fabricated, or the truth gets stretched a bit as time goes on.)

College coaches are looking for specific physical characteristics that vary from one sport to another. Universities differ from one another in their requirements, too, but each has its own grid. And if you don't fit their particular profile, some schools simply won't be interested.

Certain physical traits, unfortunately, are beyond your control. You can't change your height, for example. While you can raise or lower your weight to some degree, it's difficult to make dramatic changes in this area without affecting your balance and speed. On the other hand, if you fit the profile—for example, if you're a football lineman, 6'5" or taller, and 280 pounds or more—some colleges will do just about anything to attract you to their campuses; when an athlete has the right physical attributes, many coaches are convinced that even if there are shortcomings in his talents, they can develop him into a strong lineman (or whatever his position or sport may be) over a four- or five-year time period.

ARE YOU MAXIMIZING
YOUR PHYSICAL ATTRIBUTES?

Of course, you have no control over what college coaches think of your athletic abilities. As they judge high school athletes, they're forming subjective opinions that are completely out of your hands. Mistakes on evaluations are made every year, and there's no way for you to insure that coaches' opinions are accurate.

But you *do* have influence over many of your physical attributes, such as speed, strength, vertical jump, and agility movements. I'll describe a training program you can begin to use to move A STEP BEYOND in "cosmetic" areas like these. You'll create a training regimen that takes into account the physical demands of your particular sport. If you're not fast enough, or if you're not as strong as you'd like to be, you can do something about that. In the process, you can make sure that labels like "too slow" or "too weak" don't stick to you. And as for size, most college coaches will not discount athletes on their size alone if they have proven talents and abilities.

So don't become discouraged if you lack the "perfect" physical attributes. There are exceptions to every rule, particularly when it comes to those recruiting grids. With a little thought, you can probably assemble an all-star team of well-known players who were once overlooked but still became athletic superstars. For example, Walter Payton's size kept him from fitting the stereotype of the perfect running back, but he overcame the labels and excelled in college and professional football anyway. Brian Downing batted .240 while playing high school baseball in Southern California, but through dedication and hard work, he enjoyed a lengthy and successful career as a major league catcher and outfielder. Mugsy Bogues is just 5'4" tall—certainly not the profile of a star basketball player—but he compensated for that obvious "imperfection" with athletic talent, enthusiasm, and a great work ethic, and became an NBA star.

DEALING WITH YOUR SHORTCOMINGS

If you've got shortcomings of your own, it's important to be candid about them—with both yourself and college coaches. I've often seen young athletes fill out questionnaires and describe themselves with very impressive numbers—for example, as 6'4", 270 pounds, and a running time of 4.9 seconds in the 40-yard dash. At some point, however, colleges and coaches are going to confirm those figures. And if you're really only 6'1", 230 pounds, and have a running time of 5.6, you'll quickly find yourself *out* of the running for that school and every other one with whom you stretched the truth.

Whether you're 5'8", 6'0", or 6'2", that's what needs to go on your forms. You'll be doing yourself a disservice by reporting inaccurately. It's like saying you have a 4.0 GPA, only to have your transcript arrive indicating that it's really 2.7. The coach who sees that transcript will probably be less receptive to further information from you. But if you're honest and show respect for the recruiting process, you'll be treated fairly by most college coaches.

ABOUT YOUR WORK ETHIC—
AND OTHER INTANGIBLES

Work ethic and attitude may not be everything, but they often come very close. Although your achievements on the athletic field and in the classroom are concrete pieces of information that recruiters can evaluate, the intangibles are harder to quantify. But in my mind, they're extremely important.

Most college coaches will place a high premium on your passion for sports. Commitment, character, willpower—and, most important, heart—can overcome many cosmetic shortcomings in the eyes of coaches. These days, in fact, those qualities are almost as crucial as your ability to shoot a hook shot or hit a tennis backhand.

I met Grant Pearsall when he was a high school freshman, and there was no doubt in my mind that he would eventually be the football player of the year in his county. That was based not only on his physical talents but on his attitude and mental toughness. He loved playing and competing, and you could sense his passion from the grandstands. He also came from a great family, whose older brothers and father had all played sports.

Those personal characteristics served Grant well. While some coaches were preoccupied with just how good a player he was—analyzing his running speed and how many yards he gained during the season—they may have overlooked his great attitude both on and off the field. He is the kind of person every coach should want in the huddle. John Robinson at the University of Southern California recognized that and told him, "We may recruit a 'better athlete' than you, but we need your type of player in our program, with outstanding character as well as athletic ability." Robinson appreciated Grant for what he was—great person, great player, great student. In my opinion, Grant evolved into an outstanding athlete because of his character. He was someone who wouldn't quit, wouldn't buckle, and he helped elevate the playing level of every other athlete on his team.

At the other extreme, I've seen high school athletes who had enormous talent but very little enthusiasm for competing. While those at the top of the recruiting class rated an A for their work ethic, too many young athletes are barely pulling Cs.

RATING THE INTANGIBLES

To evaluate where you stand in the intangible factors, ask yourself:

- Am I willing to work hard to achieve my athletic goals?
- Do I aspire toward excellence, play after play, game after game, season after season?
- How committed am I to my sport over the long term?
- Am I self-motivated to improve myself athletically and in other aspects of my life, or do I need a coach or a parent to constantly push me?
- When I experience setbacks and disappointments, do I dwell on my mistakes and become easily discouraged? Or do I dust myself off and get back in the race?
- Do I believe in myself and in my ability to succeed in my sport?
- Do I get along well with my teammates and fellow athletes, and do I respect my coaches and accept their guidance and advice? As an incoming freshman, will I be able to handle starting at the bottom and competing against my teammates for playing time?

These questions can give you a sense of your passion and commitment to sports.

THE ATHLETIC SUCCESS PROFILE

To get a clear picture of whether you have "the right stuff" to play college athletics, I suggest you take the Athletic Success Profile, a computer-scored analysis that measures your athletic attitudes based on your answers to a series of questions. You'll receive a percentile ranking in eleven key areas: drive, aggressiveness, determination, responsibility, leadership, self-confidence, emotional control, mental toughness, coachability, conscientiousness, and trust. The results will graphically show you where you stand in terms of motivation within your athletic peer group and where you need to improve. The box beginning on page 25 provides descriptions of these characteristics from the Success Profile—all of which will be crucial to your college sports success.

The Athletic Success Profile has been developed over the past twenty-five years and has been used by professional, college, and Olympic teams to evaluate their current and prospective athletes. The Profile has been examined by more than fifty studies, all of which confirm its validity, reliability, and objectivity. I use the Profile with my clients, administering it to students and helping them understand the results.

The following charts show how two athletes scored on the Athletic Success Profile. I worked with both of them; they are well known and were first-round draft picks. You can see, however, how dramatically different their scores are. Only one of these athletes is still playing. Which one do you think it is? The other demonstrated an inability to cope with adversity throughout his collegiate and brief professional career and is no longer competing. Which one do you think it is?

The first chart, in fact, belonged to Shawn Green. The Toronto Blue Jays used the Profile as one tool when making the decision to draft Shawn; his results on the Profile were as impressive as his GPA, SAT, and batting average. The Blue Jays got the total package.

For more information about how you can measure your motivational skills, and to receive a comprehensive and developmental program, manual, and workbook, call the A STEP BEYOND information line, 1-800-365-9497.

ATHLETIC SUCCESS PROFILE

Student-Athlete #1

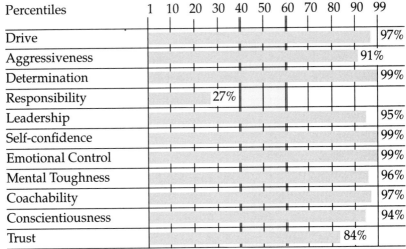

Percentiles	1	10	20	30	40	50	60	70	80	90	99	
Drive												97%
Aggressiveness											91%	
Determination												99%
Responsibility			27%									
Leadership												95%
Self-confidence												99%
Emotional Control												99%
Mental Toughness												96%
Coachability												97%
Conscientiousness												94%
Trust										84%		

Competitveness: 96% Self-control: 98% Coachability: 92% Average: 95%

Reference Group: Male, High School, Baseball   Questions Answered: 100%

Student-Athlete #2

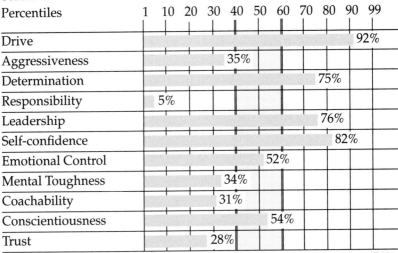

Percentiles	1	10	20	30	40	50	60	70	80	90	99
Drive										92%	
Aggressiveness				35%							
Determination								75%			
Responsibility	5%										
Leadership								76%			
Self-confidence									82%		
Emotional Control					52%						
Mental Toughness				34%							
Coachability				31%							
Conscientiousness					54%						
Trust			28%								

Competitveness: 67% Self-control: 56% Coachability: 38% Average: 54%

Reference Group: Male, High School, Football   Questions Answered: 100%

DO YOU HAVE THESE TRAITS?

You can help predict your success in sports at the college level by determining whether you possess the following personal characteristics. These qualities and their descriptions are drawn from the Athletic Success Profile,* a questionnaire that specifically measures how you rate relative to each of these traits:

Drive

Has the desire or need to win, to achieve, and to be successful in athletics; desires to attain athletic excellence; responds positively to competitive situations; aspires to accomplish difficult tasks; sets and maintains high goals in athletics.

Aggressiveness

Has the belief that taking the offensive is crucial to winning; has the tendency to initiate action and to take the offensive; releases aggression readily; is ready and willing to use force to get the job done; will not allow others to be pushy; may try to "get even" with people.

Determination

Is willing to put forth the physical effort necessary to be successful; is persistent and unrelenting in work habits; practices long and hard; works on skills until exhausted; works independently; does not give up easily on a problem.

Responsibility

Accepts responsibility for the consequences of one's actions, including mistakes; accepts blame and criticism, even when not deserved; can endure physical and mental pain; may dwell on mistakes and impose self-punishment.

Leadership

Has the desire to influence or direct others in athletics; assumes the role of leader naturally and spontaneously; enjoys the responsibility and challenge of being a leader; attempts to control the environment and to influence or direct others; makes decisions and expresses opinions in a forceful manner.

*Traits copyrighted by Institute of Athletic Motivation

Self-confidence
Possesses the belief that one has the ability needed to be successful in sports; has an unfaltering trust in self; feels sure of personal powers, abilities, and skills; handles unexpected situations well; makes decisions with assurance; is quick to express beliefs, ideas, and opinions to coaches and other athletes.

Emotional control
Has the capability to maintain composure during the stress of athletic competition; can face stress in a calm, objective manner; rarely allows feelings to affect performance; is not easily discouraged, depressed, or frustrated by bad breaks, calls, or mistakes.

Mental toughness
Has the ability to accept strong criticism and setbacks without competing less effectively; does not become easily upset when losing or competing poorly; does not need excessive praise or encouragement from the coach; recovers quickly when things go wrong.

Coachability
Has respect for coaches and the coaching process; considers receiving coaching essential to becoming a good athlete; is receptive to coaches' advice; cooperates with athletic authorities; accepts the leadership of the team captain.

Conscientiousness
Has willingness to do things according to rules; will not attempt to bend the rules to suit personal needs; has the tendency to be exacting in character and dominated by a sense of duty; places the good of the group above personal well-being; does not try to "con" the coach or other players.

Trust
Accepts and believes in people; believes what coaches and fellow athletes say; is free of jealous tendencies; tends to get along well with fellow athletes.

WHERE ARE YOU HEADED?

No matter how you fared in answering the questions in this chapter, I truly believe that there's a college right for you. Of course, some schools are more selective than others, and in any given year, many coaches may be concentrating on recruiting athletes only in particular skill positions, which may put you in—or exclude you from—the running; you might be bypassed by a certain institution simply because its needs are already met.

Some colleges recruit only in their own state, or even just in their own county, due to their own economic limitations or to talent that naturally feeds into that school. Whether the sport is basketball or baseball, track or tennis, these schools can find the athletes they need in their own backyard, and thus often look no farther than a twenty-mile radius of their campus; they'll look outside their own geographic zone only if their needs aren't being met internally. But many other colleges—including the major universities from Notre Dame to Florida State to UCLA—canvass and recruit across the nation. And most of them, whether large school or small, can provide you with a good educational and athletic experience.

Kave Galobi certainly doesn't fit the profile of the consummate football defensive back. As he entered his senior year of high school, he was undersized (5'6", 145 pounds) by traditional standards. But even at that size, he dreamed of playing college football.

Among Kave's greatest assets were his academic achievements. His GPA and test scores earned him attention in the recruiting and selection process, and he could have won acceptance to most colleges even without his sport. His work ethic and sense of commitment were impeccable, too. He wanted to attend an Ivy League college, not only for the excellent education he would receive but also because he wanted to play football there. Thanks to his academic record alone, those colleges had to take an athlete like Kave seriously. As this is being written, Kave has been accepted for admission at the University of Pennsylvania and plans to play on its lightweight football team.

BELIEVE IN YOURSELF

Later in this book, I'll guide you toward setting goals and creating strategies for yourself—athletically and academically—that can help you move successfully through the college recruiting maze. But you have to be willing to work hard to make those dreams of a college education and a sports scholarship come true. If you believe in yourself, enjoy your sport, and are involved in athletics *for yourself*—not for your parents, your girlfriend (or boyfriend), or your high school coach—there are no obstacles that can prevent you from achieving your goals.

CHAPTER 2

IMPROVING YOUR PHYSICAL PROWESS

How do high school athletes get the attention of the college coaches who can catapult them onto the campus of their choice? By becoming the most attractive candidates possible, which means making a commitment to enhance their physical skills.

RISING ATHLETIC STANDARDS

The size, speed, and performance levels of today's high school athletes are astonishing. What was considered big and fast by yesterday's *professional* standards is now considered average at the *high school* level. That's due largely to sophisticated training methods and improvements in instruction, all designed to upgrade performance. The advent of televised games and their slow-motion replays, and the analysis of expert commentators, have helped as well. And thanks to the availability of and immediate feedback provided by the videotaping of high school practices and games, coaches and players can make corrections in technique on the spot.

Hardly a day passes in which I don't hear players comment on their desire to improve their game even more. Most frequently, they describe wanting to increase their strength, power, explosiveness, speed, quickness, and/or size. Some are focused on getting better in specific situations encountered in actual games. However, when I ask them what they are doing during the off-season, for example, to reach their goals, too often the replies range from "nothing" to a description of buying a product that promised somehow to enhance speed or jumping ability. Or during that off-season, they may have decided to participate in another sport that they believed would improve their overall athletic ability. In most instances, although they're trying to move in the right direction, they really don't have a well-defined game plan or a even a target goal specific enough to get them where they want to go.

DO YOU HAVE THE ESPs?

I have refined my program to emphasize the most important qualities that athletes need to keep in the forefront of their minds. To help my players keep focused on what is important, I ask them to respond to the following: Are you *efficient?* Are you *sufficient?* Are you *proficient?* These are the crucial ESPs of my program:

Efficient: the ability to accomplish a desired effect or to perform a certain action; working properly and competently.

Sufficient: doing enough, as much as is needed, an adequate amount.

Proficient: having or showing a command in an art, skill, or area of study that allows for advancement.

THE SIX CORNERSTONES OF PHYSICAL TRAINING

To play at the college level, and to put yourself in the running for an athletic scholarship, your physical abilities in your particular sport and position need to become as fully developed as possible. With my own athletes, to help them reach A STEP BEYOND, the cornerstones of our physical training are built upon enhancing six qualities that are found in every sport that involves movement: (1) vision, (2) balance, (3) power, (4) flexibility, (5) speed, and (6) heart. (I challenge you to name a sport that does not require all six of these characteristics.) These qualities are crucial, but it takes more than a "hope it happens" attitude to improve them. The keys to success are dedication, precision, and hard work, day after day.

Think of any sport, even one as relatively obscure as archery, for example. The archer must first locate her target (which requires *vision*). Next, she must place the arrow in the center of the bow (*balance*). Then the front hand on the bow must remain locked as the opposite arm pulls the bowstring back (*power* and *flexibility*). All that remains is the release (*speed*), which propels the arrow toward its target.

The *heart* in this example is reflected in the countless hours that the archer has dedicated to familiarizing herself with her equipment and refining her skills. Her ultimate success and efficiency lie in being properly "equipped," not in the equipment itself.

Whether your own sport is football, basketball, baseball, tennis, track and field, soccer, or archery, you need to develop and refine these six basic qualities. The strategies and exercises you'll learn in this chapter are directed toward that goal. In the process, you'll increase your value in the college sports marketplace as your level of play improves.

THE RISKS OF IMPROPER TRAINING

As a young athlete, you need to spend time both on the practice field and in the weight room refining your skills. But your activities there must be conducted with care. While time in the weight room, for example, is valuable and even essential for all sports, it absolutely has to involve the *right* kind of strength training.

I was a product—and became the victim—of the "bigger and stronger" philosophy that still reigns in most of America's high schools and colleges. For as long as I could remember, the mantra I heard from coaches was, "Get bigger . . . get stronger . . . never quit." Like most young athletes, I bought into this approach. Ultimately, I could bench-press 465 pounds, squat 660 pounds, power-clean 360 pounds, run a 9.8 100 and a 4.5 40. But as impressive as those accomplishments might seem, they *didn't* improve my ability to play football. Yes, I was strong, yet as I bulked up, there was a clear erosion of my skills. I had developed muscular imbalances that interfered with my skeletal movements. As a result, my body literally fell apart, piece by piece, until the structure itself collapsed.

Here's just a partial list of my structural breakdowns: a compound fracture of the right ankle; a dislocated left ankle and torn ligament; an MCL (medial collateral ligament) tear in the left knee; three ruptured disks (third, fourth, and fifth lumbar); sciatic nerve damage; two pronged cervical vertebrae; an abdominal rupture (obliques, transverse); intestinal wall ruptures; a severed sartorius (a muscle in the inner thigh); a cracked pelvis; a fracture of the left hip; a dislocated tailbone; a broken right collarbone—and a partridge in a pear tree! All of this happened because I wanted "it" so bad. And, boy, did I get it!

Despite the injuries, I continued to play football whenever my body allowed it, almost always playing in pain. I was damaged goods at a young age, largely because of defective training techniques. As a result, my injuries eventually cut short my pro career with the Seattle Seahawks.

My story, unfortunately, isn't unique. Coaches who promote the philosophy that I bought into do develop bigger and stronger players—but these athletes don't necessarily perform better in competition. Sure, they can bench-press and squat mind-boggling amounts of weight, yet that doesn't translate into playing their game and position with greater proficiency.

WORK OUT WITH INTEGRITY

My life's mission is to show young people who want "it" precisely how to get "it" *safely*. To date, no A STEP BEYOND athlete has missed any game or performance due to any muscle-related injury!

Even as a college football coach at Stanford and San Jose State, my approach was different from a lot of my coaching colleagues. While many of them felt that "bigger is better," I never believed you should sacrifice speed for size. In the weight room, I have seen so many athletes excel on the core lifts, but as they have built bulk, they have been left feeling stiff, immobile, and unable to run and change directions as skillfully as they once could. If lifting weight has had an adverse effect on your own ability to run, throw, hit, shoot, or change direction, you need to reevaluate your program. You can lose a lot of your natural athleticism if your weight training focuses on "how much" rather than "how."

THE SENSIBLE PATH TO IMPROVEMENT

My belief is that improvement comes from experience, repetition, and refinement. To become "better" at a specific skill, you need exacting behavior and an elimination of wasted movements. Vince Lombardi, the Hall of Fame pro football coach of the Green Bay Packers and Washington Redskins, believed it took 1,000 repetitions of a particular play before it was worthy of execution in a game setting; many great teachers have a similar philosophy concerning any kind of work; to them, it's important to work hard *and* work smart.

So listen carefully to your own high school coaches when they prescribe a workout regimen—but do not assume that improvements in your size, strength, or speed will automatically produce a better performance. Too many coaches still pattern themselves after what others have done. They have a "they do it at x, y or z university, so we've got to do it here" approach—even if it isn't effective or realistic. They often hastily latch onto the latest "breakthrough" training techniques, perhaps a new Russian or Eastern European workout system, because it's being promoted as an improvement upon the existing methods. Not surprisingly, this rapid evolution in training can leave athletes confused and wondering just what they really should be doing.

Not long ago, for example, stretching before a competition became a twenty-minute routine. Then athletes were told that they needed a partner to help them perform stretching properly. Next, someone insisted that it was important to jog for a minute or two before stretching; or that a bounce was necessary while stretching. Then coaches began recommending that bouncing should be avoided altogether, relying instead on a static stretch. Without question, there will always be something still newer on the horizon that will further confuse the picture.

THE BEST APPROACH IN THE WEIGHT ROOM AND BEYOND

When making decisions about your own training program, ask yourself, "What aspects of my game do I need to improve upon?" ... "What is the purpose of lifting, and how much time should I spend in the weight room?" ... "What types of injuries (if any) have I sustained in the past year?" ... "What do I really want to accomplish in the off-season?"

Yes, many college coaches are still impressed by the image of a "bigger, stronger" athlete. A football coach may look at the raw numbers, and if a lineman is 6'5", 295 pounds, he might take a hard look at the young athlete based on those statistics alone—even if the player has trouble moving at that weight! Keep in mind that at major universities, freshmen don't usually walk on campus and immediately start at the line positions in football (or at most positions in other sports); they're usually given two to three years of seasoning before they're ready for game situations. If you've got the vital statistics they like, however, they're often willing to roll the dice that you're going to develop into someone who can play for them after the natural maturation process takes place.

Even so, no matter what your age, size, or sport, I strongly believe that your goal should *not* be to lift more just for the sake of lifting more. Walk into any weight room and you'll see lifters cheered on by their teammates yelling, "Go, you've got it, come on, don't quit!" The temptation is to lift as much as possible, even if you can't walk the next day because you overdid it and abused your body—and perhaps jeopardized your chances of ever playing another down, period, match, or game in high school or college.

So even though weight training has impacted sports performance in a positive manner in many ways, the confusion surrounding it has led some athletes to begin asking fundamental questions about its real benefits. The waters have also been muddied by many misconceptions about weight training—for example, that it stunts growth and limits flexibility—which have been proven inaccurate. In fact, *proper* weight training allows you to *improve* in these areas—and more.

Nevertheless, when I'm asked about the weight room, I tell athletes that the number one reason to lift is clear: to prevent injury! If a weight-training program is carefully planned and supervised, it can dramatically reduce your risk of injuries during competition.

Ironically, as in my own case, most sports injuries have their roots in the weight room. But your workouts really can help prevent them if you're doing things correctly. Most injuries are related to imbalances, and if you bring an imbalance within your own structure into weight training and lift in ways that your body isn't ready for, you will probably just create a bigger, stronger version of that imbalance—and a much larger injury will loom right around the corner.

When you begin a program of weight training, bear in mind that the movements you perform are much more significant than how much you lift. Do not become intimidated by peers who may have more experience or perceived strength than you, particularly when you're first starting out. Whether you're working out in a weight room on campus or in a local health club, you need to take great care to preserve your body by not trying to do too much too soon. No matter what your size and age, never use a weight you can't handle. The key to lifting is in the repetitions performed, done in a precise manner, that will contribute to improved movements in game situations.

THE CORE PROGRAM OF MOVEMENTS

It is important to understand how beautifully choreographed the movements of your body can be. To get a better picture of this, begin by looking at a door, and ask yourself what differentiates the door from a slab of wood? The answer, of course, is hinges; the hinges allow the door to open, close, and remain stable. In much the same way, our own skeletal system provides stability, and our joints permit flexion and rotation to occur. My athletes are "schooled" on these physiological principles in the same manner in which we might dissect an opponent, a play, or defensive coverage in a football game. They have an understanding that the fulcrum of their body is what we are attempting to develop, and their structural integrity will determine the degree of success or failure on any given movement.

The following movements are essential for you to begin practicing. They were developed and designed to promote balance and structural integrity within the body at all times. They are userfriendly, and are performed by all my student-athletes and teams, no matter what the sport. I suggest that you perform these movements in front of a full-length mirror each day. As you move from one position or movement to the next in this core program, follow the instructions carefully. Each exercise takes into account the structural balance of your body. All movements need to be posturally correct to avoid injuries, and they are designed to create harmony among bones, joints, ligaments, tendons, and muscles. I do not believe in stretching muscles but rather in elongating muscle groups to the exact length appropriate for their adjoining bones and joints.

INCREASE YOUR FLEXIBILITY

Fig. 1

Framing (Figure 1) This beginning position requires you to create a straight line within your body. To do this, place your feet directly under your eyes. Make sure your ankles, knees, hips, and shoulders are on parallel planes, with imaginary horizontal lines through them. Your weight should be equally distributed throughout your body frame, with the foundation of your body—your feet—supporting your entire structure. Viewing the side of your body in the mirror, check to see that you have created a vertical line through each descending joint, from shoulder to hip to knee to ankle.

Filling Up (Figure 2) This movement is designed to identify and isolate the midpoint, or fulcrum, of your body. To begin, inhale through the nostrils (keeping your mouth closed) and bring your clasped hands overhead. Feel the breathing cycle begin in your abdominals; try to inflate an imaginary basketball in your stomach from waist to rib cage.

Then exhale through your mouth, reaching upward as you do. You will feel a release in the spine and a propulsion (not explosion) of air as it moves through your chest and throat.

Repeat, experiencing a release of pressure from your lower back. This region, known as the lumbar, serves as the fulcrum as your body moves.

Fig. 2

Fig. 3

Folding (Figure 3) Inhale and bend forward at the midpoint of your body. Let your third, fourth, and fifth lumbar vertebrae act as a fulcrum as you fold forward. Position your shoulders over the toes, maintaining alignment through the ankles, knees, and hips. Then exhale and allow yourself to "drop" about an inch (bodies differ, so don't concern yourself with how far down you can go). Let your arms and hands dangle, and allow gravity to aid your movement. Hold this lowered position for five to seven seconds, return to the starting posture, and repeat three times.

Hanging (Figure 4) Widen your feet to the position depicted in the adjacent illustration. Then fold forward.

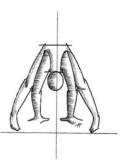

Next, place your hands on the ground directly under your eyes. Press your hands into the ground without moving forward or backward. Hold for five to seven seconds, and return to the starting position. Repeat three times.

Rotating (Figures 5–7) Begin with your feet in the same position as in the hanging posture (see Figure 4). Then bend your left arm at the elbow and rotate your left hip and left shoulder to the midpoint. Next, bend forward (fold) and place your left hand on the ground, positioning your nose over the shoelaces of your right foot. Do not twist, grab, or stretch, but rather rotate the body to a position of balance. Hold this position for five to seven seconds. Then release and repeat this process on the opposite side of the body. Break from your stance and relax.

This movement is crucial for balance when you're making a directional change while playing your sport. Your lateral muscle groups are your stabilizers and need to be incorporated in all movements. The hamstrings, gluteals, abductors, and groin are among the muscles involved in this technique.

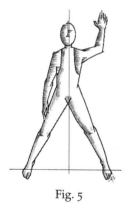

Fig. 5   Fig. 6   Fig. 7

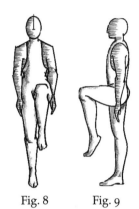

Balance Test (Figures 8–9) Begin by assuming the framing position (see Figure 1). Inhale and raise your left knee to the belt-line. Keep the left foot under the knee. Hold for five seconds. Your "down" (right) leg should be aligned through the hip, knee, and ankle. Look and feel for any instability.

Next, lower the left knee, and then raise the right knee to the belt-line, following the same procedure.

Fig. 8   Fig. 9

Archer (Figures 10–12) Assume a kneeling position as depicted in Figure 10. Maintain a straight line in the body (using your eyes and feet as a reference), keeping your left hip, knee, and ankle in alignment; the left knee should be aligned with the left eye. Your right knee (which is on the ground) should be in line with the right hip and the right ankle, under the right eye. Support your frame with your back leg and the ridges of your foot (where your toes meet the sole of the foot), directly behind your right knee. Your vision and balance are now locked in.

Fig. 10   Fig. 11   Fig. 12

Next, inhale and push forward from back to front. Place your arms straight out and then to the sides, parallel to your shoulders. This will force you to isolate your midpoint. Then raise into the archer posture, which is the final (completed) position. You will feel every muscle, joint, tendon, and ligament utilized to its full capacity.

This is the model for movement, and specifically for your first step whenever you're moving in a straight line, whether you're breaking toward the basket, approaching the tennis net, or beginning a route down the football field. Remember, your first step is contained in your stance; as an athlete, you can never regain the power of that first step if it has a structural error.

WHAT ABOUT SPORT-SPECIFIC TRAINING?

How much of your training time do you spend performing the actual activities of your sport and position? If you're like most young athletes, the answer is surprisingly little. In fact, only about *2 percent* of an athlete's off-season training is devoted to rehearsing the movements he or she will actually be performing in game situations (the other 98 percent might be spent lifting weights, climbing stadium steps, jumping off blocks, or running in a harness or a parachute, for example). And, frankly, 2 percent isn't enough if your goal is to make the leap to playing at the college level. When you think about it, how many times during a basketball game are you going to be jumping off blocks or performing an unspecified task? How many times during a football game are you going to be wearing a parachute? Frankly, I don't see the relevance of doing—and particularly *over-doing*—activities like these.

Where should you be concentrating your efforts instead? I recommend rehearsing movements in your sport to help you perform better during competition. San Francisco 49ers pass receiver Jerry Rice, for example, has created a new standard of excellence built upon a concentrated effort involving the specific tasks he performs on the football field. In much the same way, a fullback should be practicing movements he's likely to be called on to make in game situations; he'd need to practice running inside and outside plays and also track his blocking angles against specific fronts and coverages. An offensive lineman should practice not only straight-ahead movements but a battery of other movements germane to his position—such as pulling, trapping, and moving out on a sweep or a screen.

RE-CREATING THE MOVEMENTS IN YOUR SPORT

The same approach should be used by other athletes, from tennis players to soccer goalies to basketball point guards. Tennis players, for example, should choreograph their off-season training movements to coincide with segments of their game, especially those aspects perceived as weak. These might include approaching the net in a variety of circumstances that require lateral breaks of forty-five and ninety degrees to the right and to the left. This kind of training regimen will enable them to condition themselves for better performance in their sport. Advantage A STEP BEYOND!

When I work with defensive linemen, our pretraining-camp sessions involve much more than conditioning in the weight room. We spend thirty minutes on endurance, speed mechanics, and preparation for any tested events they must pass when the team arrives at camp. The next thirty to sixty minutes are devoted solely to working on physical positions (additional time may be added when maximum endurance is reached).

As part of their preparation, we simulate game situations for the defensive line positions. On the practice field, I might re-create a scenario for them, describing a specific down and distance, a particular offensive formation at the line of scrimmage, movements in the backfield and on the offensive line, and other action in the play. Instantly, they have to react to the hypothetical situation. They also practice relatively short sprints—five yards, seven yards, ten yards, fifteen yards, twenty yards—as though they were pursuing a ball carrier in an actual game circumstance. I "bombard" them with this type of situational work, and by incorporating this into their practice schedule, they have gained a distinct advantage over players who train in an unspecified manner.

For the same reasons, a baseball or softball player should practice running the bases, stealing, and scoring. In baseball, that's 360 feet of running from home plate to home plate, with left turns at each base. Yes, as a baseball player, you should be training for an improved time in the 60, since that's the distance in which you'll be timed at camps and by college and pro coaches. But for game situations, you need to be able to run the bases at full speed and negotiate the turns perfectly. Unfortunately, however, the only time most high school players run the bases in practice is when they're being punished by the coach or at the very end of practice.

I remember watching Bo Jackson in his prime, sprinting around the bases in 12.8 seconds for an inside-the-park home run. It was amazing how he hit each base with precision, never changing his stride and consistently moving the way a football back runs an option route. No drifting! No rounding! It was a 120-yard dash with three left turns. I train my baseball players the same way, rehearsing running the bases so it becomes second nature in an actual game and a form of intimidation to the defense. As Joe Morgan, the former all-star second baseman, said, "Speed never has a slump."

The key, then, is to create the movements that mirror your sport. Think of situations that have given you problems and work to solve them through your conditioning. You need to master your position. All the other effort you make won't matter if you become bigger, stronger, faster—but not better—at your particular game. Condition through your position!

Also, no matter what off-season regimen you follow, keep in mind that your performance on the field (or the court) is ultimately what is going to be evaluated by college coaches. When they review a videotape of you, they are looking for talent, not statistics. So again, concentrate on enhancing the skills required by your sport and position.

IMPROVE YOUR RUNNING

Running is a skill crucial to nearly every athlete: a sprinter emerging from the blocks, a football player coming out of his stance, a baseball player after his swing, a gymnast approaching the vault. The action is the same, the movement is consistent, no matter what the sport (swimming and water polo are two obvious exceptions).

Contrary to what some coaches believe, speed *can* be taught. But too often coaches simply assign labels to athletes they believe "can't run," are "too slow," "can't move," are "too lazy," or are "unmotivated." Chances are, you've heard these comments about players— or perhaps someone has labeled you this way.

When young athletes are instructed in running, they are often told to "explode" out of the starting blocks or the batter's box. You even hear TV sports commentators describing athletes as "exploding off the line." But that's a concept that bothers me, suggesting as it does a one-time occurrence or event. Rather, I'm looking for *perpetual movement* in an athlete, a propelling motion that involves every part of the body and continues for the duration of the play. I want *propulsion*, not explosion.

When I introduce my program to an individual or team, I typically ask, "Have you ever been beaten by just one step, whether in a race, at first base, on the goal line, or at the net?" Virtually everyone replies "yes." Then I tell them that seldom, if ever, are they beaten at the last step, but always at the *first* one. (This is why I named my company A STEP BEYOND.) As I've already pointed out, I want my athletes to understand how the body moves, beginning with the first step, and how they must take ownership over the process of athletic movement. The exercises/movements earlier in this chapter help them get off on the right foot—quite literally. And frankly, *building* speed is a misnomer; *having* speed is the goal of all those with whom I work.

THE SOURCE OF YOUR SPEED

Where does speed come from? Not from random, contrived motions. Rather, it results from a carefully choreographed sequence of movements that propels you forward with the greatest efficiency possible (think of how smoothly the arrow gets from the bow to the target). When your own movements are properly synchronized, your improvement in speed can be dramatic. The first time I work with young athletes, they eliminate a lot of wasted movement. I always time them in ten-yard increments first, knowing the importance of excelling from the starting stance to their release. After that, a 40- or 60-yard run is, in a sense, a by-product of the starting process, or the stance-release mechanism. Remember, improvement of just a tenth or even a hundredth of a second may separate victory from defeat.

Keep in mind that the urgency to cross the finish line as quickly as possible must not overshadow the important individual elements of your training. Your stance, for instance, is crucial, whether it is the archer stance depicted in Figure 12 or an adaptation of that stance for a particular sport and/or position.

In reality, then, more than teaching young people about speed, I'm teaching them about managing movement and helping them co-ordinate their bodies to function as efficiently as possible. The increases in speed are a natural by-product of the body's functioning in a synchronized manner.

If you are interested in learning more about how to dramatically improve not only your speed but also your overall movement, you can order my video, *A STEP BEYOND Training Systems: Speed Training*, by calling 1-800-365-9497.

DO YOU MEET THE COACH'S CRITERIA?

In many sports—and from one position to another in those sports—college coaches are looking for certain running speeds in their recruited athletes. Football relies on 10- and 40-yard sprints, as well as a Pro Agility or 20-yard shuttle. Baseball uses 30- and 60-yard sprints, and in some cases, running completely around the bases. Basketball, volleyball, and tennis have some form of line drills that may be timed or at least observed. (Vertical jumps are another means to measure athletic skills in a testing environment.)

Ask your high school coach about the testing standards within your sport, and prepare yourself fully to excel in these areas. In baseball's 60-yard run, for example, a time of 6.8 seconds or better will get a coach's attention.

The following grid will give you an idea of what most college football coaches look for in speed (in the 40-yard run) and size in their potential recruits. (The weight figures in particular represent low-end numbers.) Keep in mind, however, that there are always exceptions to the rule—if you are *exceptional!*

Offensive lineman	6'2"	265+ lb	5.15 to 5.65 sec
Defensive lineman	6'2"	255+	4.85 to 5.25
Fullback	5'10"	205+	4.55 to 4.80
Tailback	5'9"	180+	4.40 to 4.55
Defensive back	5'9"	175+	4.40 to 4.55
Linebacker	6'2"	220+	4.60 to 4.80
Tight end	6'3"	230+	4.65 to 4.80
Quarterback	6'3"	185+	4.65 to 4.85
Receiver	5'10"	180+	4.40 to 4.55

HOW FAST ARE YOU RUNNING?

At some point, either in letters to colleges or as part of a player questionnaire, you'll be reporting your running speed. However, when I was coaching at Stanford and San Jose State, there wasn't a single football player who gave us an accurate time in the 40. When we eventually clocked them at our camps or during the first practices, they invariably ran slower than the time they had reported. And that was a real disservice both to us and to the young athletes. When we put our own clock on every athlete, there were a lot of embarrassed young players and unhappy coaches.

To make sure you're getting as accurate a time as possible:

- Be certain you've accurately marked off the distance you're running. If you're getting timed in the 40-yard dash, take careful measurements to guarantee that you're really running 40 yards, not 35.

- Warm up for a few minutes before you're timed. If you're running cold, you're cheating yourself.

- Find someone you trust to time you. Test his skills by having him time a controlled movement. For example, at a recent pro football tryout camp, in which 400 athletes participated, our timers were asked to activate their stopwatches when I opened my hand, and then to stop their watches when I closed it; the margin of error was actually quite significant until the timers got comfortable with their own watches and their vision. We were able to eliminate as much human error as possible, eventually minimizing the differences between timers to just 2/100ths of a second.

So make sure you are timed uniformly. The timer should begin timing at your first movement, stopping the clock when the tape is hit, not before or beyond it.

- If possible, have more than one watch timing you, and record a series of three times. Before you get timed, have the timers become familiar with operating the stopwatch. If two timers have given you nearly identical times—say, 4.8 and 4.78 in the 40—you've probably gotten very accurate readings; average the two and use that as your official time.

- Electronic timing is great if the mechanisms are state of the art. Most are not, and they actually become a burden and a time-consuming apparatus. If you are timed electronically and get an accurate reading, you can expect a 2/10th-of-a-second deviation from an accurate handheld time.

- Be honest when you report your times. Eventually, college coaches are going to find out just how fast (or slow) a runner you are.

ARE YOU EATING FOR MAXIMUM PERFORMANCE?

To catch the eye of college coaches, you need to do more than work hard on the practice and playing fields and in the weight room. Your diet can be an important ally in your quest to become the best athlete you can. If you're looking for an edge, nutritional conditioning is one aspect of your training program you can't afford to ignore.

The food you consume is fuel for your body, and thus it makes sense that the right type of fuel can only enhance your body's ability to perform. On the other hand, if you're poorly nourished, you're likely to feel run down and increase your chances of injury.

Due to the sometimes overwhelming schedules most young athletes have to endure, however, rest and nutrition are frequently given the lowest priority. Massive quantities of convenience food, loaded with starch, refined sugars, high-caloric fat, and little nutritional value, become the staple for many athletes on the go. Dinner might be their only opportunity for a substantial meal, but if they're studying at the library or working out in the weight room until eight or nine at night, their evening meal might be thrown together quickly or consist of whatever they can eat standing in front of the refrigerator.

Football players and other athletes trying to increase their size might be consuming as many french fries, Twinkies, Big Macs, and sodas as possible to add pounds to their body. At the other extreme, gymnasts and wrestlers may be intentionally starving themselves, desperately trying to stay *below* a particular weight. Both behaviors can be hazardous to their health.

EVALUATING YOUR DIET

Do you even know how good or bad your diet is? As a first step, I encourage you to keep a journal of what you eat for the next week—writing down all the food you consume from morning to night, without adjusting what you normally eat. At the end of the week, a little self-analysis can tell you how well you're doing. When evaluating the journal, ask yourself these questions:

- What essentials are missing?
- Am I eating green leafy vegetables at least once a day, plus plenty of other vegetables and fruits?
- Am I eating high-protein foods like lean meat, chicken, turkey, fish, and beans?
- Do I consume dairy foods like milk, cheese, and yogurt?
- Am I getting lots of grain foods, including cereal and bread?
- Am I overdoing the candy, doughnuts, beef jerky, and fatty foods?
- Am I drinking plenty of water and juices?

IS SUPPLEMENTATION NECESSARY?

The use of nutritional supplements by athletes is a controversial area. Some coaches and sports nutritionists insist that if you eat well-balanced meals, supplementation isn't necessary. Others promote the use of pills so heavily that they ignore other aspects of nutrition.

I believe in testing rather than telling, and with the help of a physician, you can get tested to detect any problems with your intake and absorption of five minerals—iron, copper, chromium, magnesium, and zinc—that have been shown scientifically to have specific effects on athletic performance. Solid evidence now indicates that proper amounts of these minerals are crucial if your goal is to maximize your abilities and talents on the playing field. For example:

Iron is essential for transporting oxygen throughout the bloodstream, and is a critical part of myoglobin (a protein that stores oxygen reserves in muscles). Proper levels of iron help stimulate the chemical processes that produce muscle contractions. One study of 113 male and female runners found that 56 percent of them suffered from systemic iron deficiency.

Copper plays a crucial role in the body's proper utilization of iron. If your body is copper deficient, you are more susceptible to anemia. The proper development of your ligaments and tendons may also be impaired by copper shortages.

Magnesium is needed by muscles to function properly, helping them relax and promoting endurance. Specifically, a magnesium shortage impairs the movement of oxygen to muscle tissue. This mineral is also crucial for many other energy-dependent processes to occur. Magnesium helps activate the more than three hundred enzymes in the body that permit cells to function efficiently and carbohydrates and other nutrients to be utilized properly.

Zinc is important for efficient enzyme activity in the body, including those enzymes that keep lactic acids (the so-called fatigue acids) from accumulating. Zinc is also necessary for proper body growth. If you are zinc deficient, the strength and endurance of your muscles will suffer, as will your body's ability to efficiently repair tissue. Zinc (as well as magnesium) supplements should be taken after dinner and before bedtime, since most muscle growth and repair take place during sleep, and levels of these minerals will be highest if they're consumed late in the day. A recent study found that increases in zinc intake significantly improved muscle performance in athletes.

If you're deficient in **chromium**, energy metabolism will suffer. Chromium stimulates the proper activity of the hormone insulin, which moves glucose into your muscle cells, promoting muscle development and growth. One study of runners found that their loss of both chromium and zinc in the urine was 50 to 100 percent greater on run days, compared to nonrun days.

Athletes deficient in one or more of these five minerals can experience a variety of problems that impair performance—from muscle fatigue to cramping, from night sweats to insomnia.

GETTING RELIABLE NUTRITIONAL ADVICE

Most young athletes are unclear about where to turn for nutritional help. They often fall prey to clever marketing campaigns and product packaging, which usually feature a prominent athlete's name and image, and that offer nostrums and advice of questionable scientific validity. Still, with a "monkey-see-monkey-do" mentality, it's easy to lapse into thinking, "If Athlete X takes it, it must be good!" And if a little is good, they say, a lot must be even better.

When it comes to nutrition, I urge you to be guided by scientific research, not testimonials. A personalized nutritional approach, based on findings from *your* blood and *your* urine, makes the most sense. You should have an objective measure of your own nutritional strengths and needs. Based on the results of these tests, a nutritional program can be designed specifically for you, which may include supplementation.

My advice is to discuss this issue with your physician. I have also found the use of a testing process created by BALCO (Bay Area Laboratory Co-op) particularly useful. Evaluating blood and urine samples, BALCO's technology can provide you with an individualized report on where your own nutritional deficiencies (if any) lie, but you'll need a physician to order the tests and perhaps help you interpret BALCO's findings. For more information, call 1-800-777-7122.

THE PERILS OF STEROIDS

We live in a time when everyone is looking for a quick fix, a miracle food, or a shortcut. But there are no magic pills or potions that will help you grow from 5'8" to 6'2" overnight, or instantly allow you to hit a baseball farther than Ken Griffey Jr. or Frank Thomas.

Undoubtedly, you've heard a lot about steroids. Despite all their negative publicity, they are widely available, and are used by athletes in their teens and twenties eager for an advantage over the competition. Steroids are derivatives of the male hormone testosterone, but their use is not only illegal, it is also potentially life-threatening. Lyle Alzado, the all-pro defensive end, believed that steroids caused his fatal brain cancer, while the detection of steroids forced sprinter Ben Johnson to forfeit his gold medal in the 1988 Olympic Games. Nevertheless, athletes obsessed with an "I've got to get bigger" mentality have tunnel vision that allows them to become blind to the risks of devastating side effects, including liver tumors, a weakened immune system, abnormalities in the sexual organs, mood swings ("'roid rages"), and suicidal tendencies.

In addition to steroids, other illegal drugs—as well as alcohol and cigarettes—are very accessible, and will impair athletic performance and undermine an otherwise healthy nutritional program. If you're thinking about using any of these substances, think again. Yes, steroids may build bigger muscles, but they're a shortcut to physical, emotional, and social ruin. You have everything you need already contained within your own body and mind; don't look outside for what already exists within.

GUIDING YOUR OWN DESTINY

My coaching philosophy has always been that *you*—much more than your coaches, your parents, or your teammates—are responsible for your success on and off the athletic field. The latest training gimmick or the newest performance-enhancing drug cannot make you better—but *you* can. *You're* going to get accepted to college if *you* are willing to do the things prescribed in this book. So you need to take responsibility for your own present and future. It's that simple.

CHAPTER 3

YOUR ACADEMIC GAME PLAN

Most of the college recruiting process is exciting and even glamorous. Imagine yourself being invited to visit the campus of a college you've always dreamed of attending. Or visualize yourself answering the phone and hearing the voice of a college coach you've always admired, talking to you about coming to her school. Or picture a letter arriving from a university to which you've applied, notifying you that you're being offered a scholarship.

But to get to the position where you're a winner in the recruiting game, you need to put in hard work and long hours—and not just on the practice and playing fields. Your accomplishments in the classroom are a crucial part of the overall profile college coaches and admissions personnel evaluate, and you can't afford to neglect them.

PUTTING ACADEMICS IN PERSPECTIVE

As I'll stress throughout this book, there's a lot about recruiting that is governed by purely subjective judgments beyond your control. One college coach may see you play high school football and be impressed by your agility, pursuit, and tackling prowess. But another coach may watch the same game and conclude that your performance is only average, and shows little potential for improvement. Those impressions are simply one person's judgment, and you have no control over whether he or she considers you a blue-chip recruit or an also-ran. Sometimes those evaluations are right on target, but errors are made all the time, and there's really nothing you can do about it.

But there's no room for subjectivity when it comes to your academic record. Your grades are on your transcript in black and white, and if you've excelled—if you have a 3.0 or 3.5 grade point average, for example—it can set you apart from the pack. Remember, there are six million high school students playing sports, and that academic transcript can give you an important edge if it shows a commitment to excellence *off* the field, too.

MAKING GRADES A PRIORITY

If you haven't already done so, you need to make grades your top priority. No matter how good an athlete you are, your schoolwork matters, and, in many cases, will determine just how interested a particular college is in you. I work only with student-athletes, not just athletes. As I tell these young people, if they haven't dedicated themselves to succeeding in the classroom, they're cheating themselves out of an important part of life that will serve them well not only in their pursuit of a college scholarship but for many decades to come. My student-athletes have a cumulative GPA (grade point average) of 3.5 (on a 4.0 scale); with grades like that, no wonder we have achieved 100 percent college placement.

Coaches recognize the challenges they face during recruiting, and academics can be the toughest hurdle. A student's attitude in the classroom often is the ultimate factor determining whether he gets into a four-year college, and how well he'll do once he gets there. Too often, prospects are "all dressed up" with nowhere to go; they may shine on the athletic field, but it doesn't mean much if they haven't taken the right classes in high school, haven't taken the proper tests, or if poor grades have eliminated them from consideration by four-year colleges. The standardized tests may be a challenge, but if you work hard and prepare yourself, you can do well on the SAT/ACT tests, as well as earn a good GPA. You *can* control your academic destiny.

DO YOU MEET THE NCAA REQUIREMENTS?

In admitting student-athletes, colleges are bound not only by their own admissions requirements but also by the academic eligibility guidelines created by the National Collegiate

Athletic Association (NCAA). These criteria are revised peri-odically, so you need to keep up to date on the latest man-dates, including the specific classes you must take in high school.

In Appendix B (see page 169), you'll find the 1996–97 re-quirements in effect when this book was written. The NCAA can send you a free booklet describing its latest rules and reg-ulations for high school students with their sights set on playing college sports. Ask for *NCAA Guide for the College-Bound Student-Athlete* by writing or calling the NCAA (6201 College Blvd., Overland Park, KS 66211; (913) 339-1906).

WHERE ACADEMIC EXCELLENCE REALLY PAYS OFF

It's never too early to start getting your academic life in order. As far as colleges are concerned, your grades start to count beginning in your sophomore year (tenth grade) of high school. But I firmly be-lieve that the sooner you adopt good study habits, the better. By the time your grades really matter, you should already have laid the aca-demic groundwork so getting A's and B's is a habit. If you're used to setting aside time each night to do homework, and have learned how to study for exams, you won't be shocked by having to shift gears in the tenth grade and really apply yourself for the first time.

The bottom line: Good grades count, no matter what college you want to attend. But they are a particularly precious commodity if you're aiming toward a school where an excellent academic record is an absolute necessity. Keep in mind that the NCAA criteria that you'll find in Appendix B are the *minimum* requirements; but at some universities, those ground-floor GPA and SAT scores won't get even a moment's attention in the admissions office.

WHAT ABOUT THE ELITE COLLEGES?

Perhaps you can throw a fastball at ninety miles per hour, or dunk a basketball like Michael Jordan. But that won't mean a thing to the nation's most prestigious universities if you haven't excelled in the classroom. These colleges include Stanford, Northwestern, Duke, the Ivy League schools (Harvard, Yale, Princeton, Dartmouth, Columbia, Cornell, Penn, and Brown), and the service academies (Army, Navy, Air Force). Coaches at these colleges can recruit *only* those athletes who are also academic standouts.

That may be discouraging if you have your sights set on one of these schools, since if you have a 2.0 or a 2.5 GPA, you're not going to impress their coaches. Nevertheless, there's another side to the story: If you can get your academic life on the fast track—and raise your GPA to a 3.2, 3.5, or 3.8, for example—you'll have a tremendous advantage in the eyes of these colleges, compared to most of your graduating class. In fact, if you're at the top of your game academically, you can be recruited by virtually any college in the country—and by combining both athletic talent and academic achievement, colleges like the Stanfords and the Dukes *have* to pay attention to you.

There's a misconception that unless you have a GPA of 4.0—or higher—there's no way that these prestigious universities will even give you a second look. But that's not true if you're an athlete, since admissions offices will bend a bit. Yes, for the nonathlete, these schools are typically looking for students with a 4.0 GPA and 1400 on the SATs. But they have a little more latitude for "athletic admits," and so if you carry a 3.5 or 3.75 GPA, for example, you're probably right in the ballpark and quite "presentable"—and one of the few athletes they can recruit.

Sports, then, can serve as a launching pad to help you gain admission to one of the country's finest institutions, even if you don't have a straight-A average. But with both good grades and athletic skills, you're really one of a select group of potential recruits. After all, how many high school students can bat .375 *and* earn a 3.75 GPA? Or average twenty points per basketball game, *and* have a 3.6 GPA? When I was an assistant football coach at Stanford University, there were nationally an average of only about thirty-five high school students per year who were top-notch athletes who also fit our academic profile. These were the only young men we could realistically talk to—and they were also being courted by other prestigious athletic/academic institutions. The very good athletes with very good grades had enormous leverage and control over where they would go to college.

MAXIMIZING YOUR POTENTIAL

Even if you aren't aiming for a school like Stanford or Duke, and even if it seems like a 3.8 GPA just isn't within your reach, you can still use academics to your advantage by boosting your GPA as high as possible. If you're now a 2.5 student, raising it to 3.0 can broaden your college horizons significantly, while also showing your willingness and commitment to do the academic work in a mature manner.

As I've said earlier, your performance in the classroom is a factor you *can* control. You can't influence the college coach who looks at you on the softball field with skeptical eyes, thinking, "She can't play for us; she's not fast enough." But you *can* take charge of the circumstances that may ultimately force that same coach to say, "Well, she does have a 3.6 GPA, 1100 on the SATs, and she works so hard on the field. Maybe she does deserve an opportunity."

If you have all the cosmetic virtues—height, weight, speed, athletic ability, *and* grades—you're on the road to a college of your choosing, and perhaps with a scholarship in hand. But if your grades aren't where you want them to be—or if you haven't taken the right courses and met even these most basic academic requirements—you'll have *nowhere* to go, except perhaps to a junior college. If you find yourself asking, "Why aren't I being asked to the dance?"—it might be because you didn't live up to your academic potential.

DO NOT SELL YOURSELF SHORT

Don't buy into the "dumb jock" image; it's a stereotype that doesn't apply to the young athletes I work with. Even if you've never excelled on your report card, it's important not to underestimate yourself and what you can accomplish. If you're a football player, just think about everything you've had to learn and remember, game after game. If you play free safety, for example, you have had to memorize a number of defensive formations and their hieroglyphic names ("Eagle G cover 2"). In each of those formations, you need to know not only your own responsibilities but those of your ten teammates. You must adapt quickly to a variety of game circumstances: down-and-distant situations, playing on the short side of the field. You've learned how to read the second receiver out of the backfield to determine the depth of your drop, and you've learned to evaluate the quarterback's movements and launch point. You're processing a lot of information—and probably doing it well, one play after another.

That should prove to you that you *do* have the ability to listen, understand, and assimilate information. You can follow instructions and take direction. You've shown you can do it on the athletic field; now it's time to do it in the classroom, too.

You're fortunate: Still in high school, you have time to make your grades count, to turn them into one of your greatest assets, and not just slide through, devoting most or all of your energies to sports. In my own life, I was a late bloomer academically, and it took Dr. Norma Eichhorn, one of my professors at San Jose State, to finally wake me up. During my senior year, she took me aside and said, "Jim, you're not going to get away with it. It's time to apply yourself and take this schoolwork seriously." It was the first time someone had ever done that—and perhaps with a little maturity under my belt, I took her seriously. I committed myself to spending forty hours a week, spread out over all seven days, in the library. The first week, I hated it. But by the second week, I began to see signs that it was paying off. By the third week, I couldn't wait to crack the books. During the fourth week, I was telling myself, "Boy, did I get ripped off! I really missed out on a lot of education, trying to cram an entire semester into two nights' work."

Later in this book, I'll guide you through the steps you'll take to make contact with college coaches and recruiters. And I'll recommend that when you or your parents write letters to those universities, you include an unofficial high school academic transcript and, if you've taken the SAT or ACT, a copy of those scores. If you're really serious about a college scholarship and playing sports at a four-year institution, the more impressive your academic records look, the better you'll be perceived at those colleges.

A COMMITMENT TO ACADEMIC SUCCESS

No matter what your grades are today—whether you're a B, C, or D student—there's room for improvement. Starting today, commit yourself to making your schoolwork your number-one priority.

Keep in mind, however, that there are no quick fixes, no shortcuts, and no gimmicks when it comes to academics. You'll have to work as hard in the classroom and at your desk at home as you do on the athletic field.

As a first step, ask yourself the following questions:

- Where do my grades stand right now?
- What's my GPA?
- Can I take my grades from where they are now and move them up to the next level? Am I willing to put in the extra hours to achieve the improvements I need to make?
- Am I willing to set high academic goals for myself and do what's necessary to achieve them?

I hope you answered "yes" to the last question. No matter what your academic transcript currently shows, you can probably make it look better. But it will take self-discipline, a powerful work ethic, and a sincere commitment to make a positive change in your academic achievements.

While you can't reach the top of the academic mountain overnight, you can set some achievable mini-goals, and attain each of them. It might not be realistic that you can raise your overall GPA from a 2.8 to a 3.8 in a single semester; but you may be able to raise it to 3.2 this semester, and then to 3.4 the next, and so on.

Of course, there will be times when you'd rather be socializing than studying. But take a few moments each day to evaluate your passion to play college sports. Keep that vision in mind, and create a "must-do" attitude for your schoolwork.

KEEPING ON TRACK ACADEMICALLY

You need to excel in the classroom, not just in your athletic uniform. Here are steps you can take, beginning now, to help insure that you'll achieve your dreams:

- Take the high school classes that will meet the NCAA requirements to qualify you to play sports in college. (See Appendix B for the required core classes, and then work with your guidance counselor to make sure you will take all of them by the end of your senior year.)

- Go to class—every class, every day. When you're there, listen carefully, and take good notes.

- Buy a day planner and record every homework assignment and when it's due. Write down the dates of tests, and don't wait until the night before to begin studying. When term papers are assigned, work on them a little at a time, rather than trying to do it all just before they're due.

- Set aside a quiet place—in your room or in another part of the house—where you can study every night. Keep your goals in mind, turn off the TV, and hit the books. Complete every homework assignment and turn it in on time. Study for every test for as long as it takes to feel comfortable with the material.

- Improve your time-management skills. During your sports season in particular, you need to make the best use of your time, insuring that you set aside enough time to study each night. If you have a twelve-page reading assignment in your history class—and you know it takes you five minutes to read and absorb the material on each page—schedule a full hour to do the reading. That may mean passing up an invitation from your friends to "hang out" when you have a test the next day. But keep your eyes on the prize, and what's really important.

- Meet frequently with your teachers. Part of their job is to make themselves available—during office hours, for example—to give you extra help when you need it. Know what your grades are at all times. Let your teachers know how serious you are about raising your grades. Ask them, "What do I have to do to get an A or a B in this class? Are there extra-credit assignments I can do to help my grade?"

- If you need assistance beyond what your teacher can provide, ask your guidance counselor if on-campus tutoring is available, perhaps provided by other students at little or no cost. Or request a referral to a private tutor.

- Take a class or two in summer school. Summer is a time to take particularly hard classes, since you can devote more time to them without the burden of other courses— and your athletic season.

- Sign up to take the SAT or ACT. I recommend that you take this standardized test for the first time in your junior year (you can take it more than once). You'll not only become familiar with the test but if your scores are not as high as you would like, you'll have plenty of time to take it again. Also, if you have good SAT/ACT scores and can provide them early to college coaches who may have interest in you, it will show them during the initial stages of recruiting that you are a viable candidate worth pursuing. (You can also get used to these standardized tests by taking the PSAT—Practice SAT—which many students take in their sophomore or junior year.)

- If you need to raise your scores on the SAT or ACT test, explore the alternatives that can help you do better the next time you take it. Your own high school may have a course you can take (after school or on Saturdays) designed to improve your test-taking performance. Books are available in the library and bookstores that provide SAT/ACT instruction and practice tests. Independent services (such as the Princeton Review, Kaplan Test Prep) offer courses designed to boost your test scores.

- Inquire about your need to take the SAT II tests. Some colleges require you to submit your scores on these SAT

IIs, which are exams that concentrate on a particular topic (English, American history, Spanish, mathematics, etc.). Ask your high school counselor about what SAT II tests you may need to take.

- Seek the support of your parents in your academic pursuits. Can they drive you to the library when necessary? Will they help keep your siblings quiet so you can study at night? If you need a tutor, can they help you find (and fund) one?

KEEPING TRACK OF YOUR GRADES AND SCORES

Most athletes can tell you their softball batting average or the tackles-per-game they've averaged on the football field. But they should be just as familiar with how they're doing in the classroom. Use a chart like this one to keep track of your high school academic achievements in which colleges are most interested:

Grade Point Average

	Overall	Core Classes
My sophomore year GPA:	_____	_____
My junior year GPA:	_____	_____
My senior year GPA:	_____	_____

SAT/ACT

Date taken: _____ Score: _____
Date taken: _____ Score: _____
Date taken: _____ Score: _____

SAT II

Test subject: _____ Date: _____ Score: _____
Test subject: _____ Date: _____ Score: _____
Test subject: _____ Date: _____ Score: _____

USING ACADEMICS TO REACH YOUR GOALS

Remember, the classroom can become one of your most powerful allies in your pursuit of an athletic scholarship. It is important to appreciate learning just for the sake of learning—but it can also help you achieve many goals in your life.

A final thought: One of the most encouraging trends in college sports today is the emergence of the student-athlete who has finished undergraduate courses and begun postgraduate studies before the completion of his or her sports eligibility. These are young athletes who take their work in the classroom very seriously and fully recognize its value. You, too, can maximize your education if you choose to take your academic life—in high school and in college—A STEP BEYOND.

CHAPTER 4

BUILDING MENTAL TOUGHNESS

Your personal attributes and qualities—height, weight, speed, strength, vertical jump, and agility—are easy to measure. Much harder to quantify, yet just as important, are your mental perseverance, your passion, and your heart.

A tough and positive mental outlook is crucial to your success in sports, in the classroom, and in the race toward college and a possible athletic scholarship. If you have heart, and a willingness to sacrifice and work hard, you can significantly boost your standing in the eyes of college coaches.

THE SOURCE OF YOUR TOUGHNESS

Your mental toughness, of course, has to come from within. It's an attitude, and it can't be developed by performing the proper exercises in the weight room, or by eating the right foods. Sure, a coach's pat on the back feels great, but maintaining consistent mental intensity—practice after practice, play after play, game after game—has its origins internally.

We've all seen athletes with courage. They go beyond what appear to be their physical limitations, driven by desires of the *heart* when their bodies seem underdeveloped, overmatched, or "broken." Their passion for their sport is deep within their being. They are purposeful, focused, and consumed with fulfilling their goals.

A CASE OF COURAGE

I sometimes think that when it comes to courage, David Wyman created the mold. In the mid-1980s, he suffered one of the most severe football injuries I've ever witnessed. Playing for Stanford in a game at the University of Arizona, he took a fierce block on the joint of his left knee. In an instant, his knee tore and shattered. It suffered dislocations. Tendons and ligaments were severed. As he was carried from the field, his lower leg was almost at a right angle to his upper leg. Doctors said it looked as though he had been in the worst kind of motorcycle accident. Shortly after the injury, one orthopedic surgeon said he wasn't even sure if all of David's leg could be saved.

Fortunately, when David awoke from surgery, his leg was intact, but he was emotionally devastated. His football career was in serious jeopardy, although he had even more basic concerns. "Jim," he told me, "I just want to walk again."

David was very tough, and I believed he could work a miracle in rehab. While he was still in the hospital, I got his game jersey, took his name off the back, and substituted the word COMEBACK in its place. I handed it to David in his hospital bed and told him what I thought he could accomplish.

Yes, there were times when David doubted his ability to "come back." Early in his rehab at Stanford, he told me, "Jim, it's just not working; I'm not getting it done here." So we set him up with one of the top rehab specialists in the country, and he immersed himself in a high-intensity program aimed not just at getting him in shape to play again but also directed at restoring his confidence and giving him a choice about whether he *wanted* to return. He began with sets of fifty repetitions of squats with no weight, which eventually evolved into real challenges in the weight room. He rode a mountain bike at high altitudes over rugged courses. He also was guided through the mental and emotional sides of coming back—a big part of the rehab process. He spent hours in the coaches' offices, studying game films and adopting a mindset of playing again. He never gave up. He never quit.

Ultimately, David conquered the biggest hurdle of all by being willing to risk reinjuring his knee. He returned to the football stadium at Stanford and became one of our most outstanding players. In the ensuing years, David has spent nine years in the National Football League, driven as much by desire as by his enormous talent.

HOW TOUGH-MINDED ARE YOU?

To catapult yourself from the high school gymnasium to a major college arena, you need not only physical talent but also those intangibles like mental toughness. So how do you rate in this critical area? Do you have what it takes?

To answer those questions, a good place to start is to turn to chapter 1 ("Undergoing a Reality Check") and review how you responded to the following queries:

"Am I willing to work hard to achieve my athletic goals?"

"Am I self-motivated to improve myself athletically and in other aspects of my life, or do I need a coach or a parent to constantly push me?"

"How committed am I to my sport over the long term?"

Here are some additional questions to help you evaluate your passion and your mental toughness:

"Am I usually the last one to leave the practice field, willing to work a little longer than my teammates to refine my skills?"

"Am I able to stay focused during each game, concentrating fully on every play, or do I often find myself daydreaming or drifting mentally?"

"When my team is losing a game, rather than allowing myself to feel defeated, do I turn inward to find something extra that allows me to play even harder to pull out a victory?"

"Do I always strive for excellence?"

"Do I really want to be a champion?" (By definition, a champion is a fighter for a noble cause—and that noble cause should be your commitment to your academic and athletic lives.)

If you answered "yes" to these questions, you have a passion for your sport that can dramatically improve your chances for an athletic scholarship. Of course, we all have days when we'd prefer to turn off the alarm clock and return to sleep rather than dive into the swimming pool for practice before dawn. But that feeling should be fleeting and uncommon. You must recognize that a disciplined work ethic is one of your greatest strengths.

THE CORNERSTONES OF SUCCESS

In chapter 2, I introduced you to the cornerstones of A STEP BE-YOND's physical-training program, which is built upon a foundation of enhancing your vision, balance, power, flexibility, speed, and heart. As crucial as these qualities are to your physical development, there is also a mental side to each of them that is equally important to your overall success.

Vision: Sharp, focused vision allows you to see where you want to go at all times. Keep your eyes on the prize, whether it's a victory in the next game or the more distant dream of playing at the college level. That vision will be a guiding light that helps you make decisions in your own best interest; for example, when friends tempt you with party plans on the night before a midterm exam, are you committed enough to tell them that your social life will have to wait for another evening when you don't have to study?

Balance: In striving toward your goal, you need to maintain a balance. Work hard and steadily toward your dream, but without going to extremes where you unnecessarily risk injury or burnout. You also need to lead a balanced life where academics get as much attention as sports. Eat properly, and keep your mind fresh and relaxed by finding time for adequate sleep and a social life.

Power: Power is a reflection of your inner strength and conviction—qualities that are necessary to ride through the peaks and valleys on the path to college admission.

Flexibility: When your fourth-quarter pass is intercepted, or you strike out with the winning run at third, you need the flexibility and determination to hang tough, despite your disappointment, and the resilience to start again. Bend, maybe—but break never!

Speed: Work toward your goal with all the engines in high gear and the energy surging—without racing recklessly and out of control toward the finish line.

WHAT ABOUT HEART?

Your heart is your life source. It will help you deal with the tough times, sweep away the obstacles, and grab an edge over the competition when it once didn't seem possible.

Every college team, no matter what the sport, has that special breed of player who makes up in heart what he or she may lack in physical prowess—the second baseman hitting only .230, but who expends more blood, sweat, and tears than anyone on the field . . . the volleyball player who may not leap as high as some of her teammates but who has an unwavering work ethic and who has jettisoned the word "quit" from her vocabulary. Those qualities will keep you hustling when it would be easier to give up; at the same time, it can boost your worth to college coaches who make the decisions that could affect your future.

Without question, heart can also help you weather the storms that are an inevitable part of the college recruiting game. Egos can soar or be crushed in the course of a phone call or a letter from a college coach. You need to be able to enjoy the applause and the adrenaline rushes, as well as rebound from the disappointments. You can learn valuable lessons from the setbacks, the misevaluations, and the injuries, as long as you don't let them overwhelm or crush your spirit. No one wants to be told that a particular college coach has lost interest in him or her, but it's part of sports. It will hurt for a while, but if you have your head and your heart connected, you'll recover and look forward to the next challenge.

THE PAYOFF OF A "NO-QUIT" ATTITUDE

One of the most inspiring young athletes I've worked with is Tim Lavin. Not only did Tim have exceptional skills as a running back, but he had a passion for football that kept him focused and determined. After high school, he wanted desperately to play at the University of Southern California, and when he wasn't offered a scholarship, he became a walk-on there. He knew the scholarship players would be offered every opportunity to prove they could play before he would ever be given a chance. But he remained confident while spending one year, then the next, on the scout team at USC, a position with little status and even fewer rewards.

Frankly, most young players would have eventually thrown up their hands, growing weary of feeling more like a tackling dummy than an athlete. But Tim persevered, endured the drudgery, and kept a strong vision of his ultimate goal of playing on Saturday afternoon for USC. Repeatedly, he was named Scout Team Player of the Week —so often, in fact, that the coaches decided they could no longer give him that award. Still, on game days, Tim remained on the sidelines, suited up but never playing.

Frustrated but still keeping his dream alive, Tim pleaded his case to the USC coaching staff. He believed he had proven himself to the coaches as being "worthy" of receiving a scholarship. Finally, in good conscience, the coaches agreed. They acknowledged his talents as a player—and they granted him a full scholarship and a place on the team. Tim's mental toughness had paid off. He never quit, he ended up putting on the USC uniform and playing on special teams, and he was the leading rusher in the game against Utah State.

OVERCOMING OBSTACLES

In high school, if you've had a bad game—perhaps thrown a few interceptions and been sacked too many times—put it aside as soon as possible, and don't let your confidence waver. Yes, self-doubts are part of life, but if you've got a strong work ethic, you can overpower them. Like an actor who experiences stage fright, you might feel a little shaky in your first game after a bad outing, but get back into the fray. To me, a player isn't a failure just because he has moments without glory; he fails only if he gives up and stops trying.

Shawn Green, for example, overcame many obstacles before earning a regular spot in the starting lineup of the Toronto Blue Jays. He signed a blue-ribbon contract with the Blue Jays right out of high school. Expectations were so high, and so many eyes were on him, that Shawn couldn't help but feel enormous pressure. In his first year in the minors, things couldn't have been much more frustrating. He hit .230—and broke his thumb. The pressures intensified, and the disappointment became increasingly difficult to accept.

But Shawn never relinquished his vision of what he wanted to achieve. Put in perspective, the fractured thumb was only a small hurdle in his path to the major leagues. He kept his dream alive, and today he's playing in "The Show," and is destined to become an all-star-caliber player.

MOLDING A POSITIVE MINDSET

In your mind, begin painting a picture of the reality you want. Does it include being the best player on your high school team? Raising your grades to the highest levels they've ever been? Gaining admittance to the college of your choice? Winning an athletic scholarship? Wearing a college football (or basketball or softball) uniform and helping your team win game after game?

Once you've set these goals, work at creating the attitude "If I want to accomplish something, I can." Don't let anyone tell you that your dream is beyond reach. (Remember the movie *Rudy* and the young Notre Dame walk-on who overcame seemingly insurmountable odds and hardships to fulfill his dreams?) Figure out all the small steps you need to take to reach your goals, and make each of those steps a priority. Take control of the situation. Be willing to make sacrifices, and you'll be surprised at what you can accomplish.

Terri McKeever, the women's swimming coach at the University of California at Berkeley, acknowledges that college coaches, of course, are interested in your athletic talents. But most coaches are looking for more, she says, including a positive attitude and a strong work ethic. "The most important attribute a student-athlete can bring to our team is who she is as a person," says Terri. "Her swimming abilities and academics are very important. But I'm also looking for athletes who have good skills in dealing with people, who are willing to be coached, and who are good learners."

KEEPING YOUR DREAMS ALIVE

Gerald Wilhite is one of those amazing athletes whose personal qualities and courage refused to let his dreams die. In high school, he was a gymnast and a wrestler, but weighed less than a hundred pounds as a freshman. Toothpick-thin through most of his adolescence, he finally "bulked up" to about 115 pounds by graduation.

Gerald went to junior college, where he began playing football with the goal of taking his love for the sport as far as he could. With a backbreaking work ethic, he built himself up to 170 pounds, excelled on the playing field, and was recruited by some of the top four-year universities in the country. Gerald accepted a scholarship from San Jose State University but, like David Wyman, became side-lined by a terrible knee injury. I remember pointing at the scar on my own knee, and telling Gerald, "Don't listen to the negatives associated with your injury; you can make it all the way back, but you're going to have to bust your rear end to do it."

Gerald did. His knee healed, and in his senior year, he became the second back in NCAA history to run for 1,000 yards and catch fifty or more passes in one season. In the pro draft, he was a first-round draft pick, and he ended up having a long and superb career with the Denver Broncos.

Gerald could have given up in high school, convinced that his size was an overwhelming obstacle to playing football in college (not to mention the pros). But he believed in himself, and so did his family. He worked as hard as any athlete I've ever met. He had a great heart, and it carried him all the way to the NFL.

Gerald wasn't the only story of amazing perseverance to come out of San Jose State. Gil Byrd graduated from Lowell High School in San Francisco, and became a walk-on running back at San Jose State. He impressed the coaching staff with his toughness and athletic ability, and the next year, he was switched to the defensive back position.

In his sophomore year, however, while playing a road game at the University of California, Gil caught his foot in the carpet of the artificial turf, and blew out his knee—an injury so severe that, particularly in those days (the early 1980s), it usually ended careers. But Gil fought back. He got himself back into playing shape, and eventually had such an outstanding college career that he became a first-round NFL draft pick, playing for years with the San Diego Chargers, and earning the reputation as a great pass interceptor, a ferocious hitter, and a certain Hall of Famer. All because he believed in himself and was unwilling to let anyone stand in his way of achieving his goals.

ARE YOU WILLING TO MEET THE CHALLENGE?

The athletes I've mentioned here—including Gil, Gerald, and David (as well as myself)—were helped tremendously in our recoveries by great doctors like Martin Trieb and Don Bunce (Don is also a former Rose Bowl quarterback with Stanford's 1972 team). But the personal qualities of these athletes helped tremendously, too, including a tough and positive attitude and a powerful desire to play—characteristics that kept them focused during their long battle back.

If you have this kind of outlook as well, it will not only serve you well in high school and college sports, but also in the years ahead. If you have heart . . . if you're willing to sacrifice and work hard to succeed . . . you can deal successfully with the most demanding situations and greatest challenges you'll encounter the rest of your life.

One additional thought: As you formulate your own dream and pursue it with the highest degree of mental toughness, make sure that it's really *your* dream. Too many parents put too much pressure on their children to perform, perhaps as a way of living out their own desires through their kids or to gain some recognition for themselves in the community. If you're pursuing someone else's dreams, not your own, it's eventually going to show up in the quality of your play. Compete because *you* want to, not because someone else is pushing you.

PART II

INSIDE THE RECRUITING PROCESS

CHAPTER 5

THE RECRUITING BEGINS

College recruiting is a system in perpetual motion. Hour after hour, day after day, virtually around the clock, it never rests. Because it is so fast moving, if you aren't knowledgeable about how the process works, you can get left behind as colleges evaluate young athletes and select those to whom they'll make offers.

From the student's and parents' point of view, the recruiting process can be intimidating and shrouded in mystery. "When I recruit, one of my jobs is to fill students in on what to expect, and how the whole process works," says David Tipton, football recruiting coordinator and defensive line coach at Stanford University. "Frankly, a lot of students and their families are clueless about recruiting when the process begins, yet they know that there's a huge decision ahead that they're going to have to make. So we try to educate them."

This chapter and the ones that follow will help you understand recruiting, its ground rules and timetables, how colleges and coaches play the recruiting game, and the way students and parents can navigate successfully through this complicated maze. As you'll see, it's not enough to sit back and wait for the phone to ring. You need to become a proactive participant in the process.

A PERSONAL STORY: THE ECSTASIES AND AGONIES OF RECRUITING

Years ago, when I was a high school student, I discovered that recruiting isn't an exact science, nor is it always enjoyable, particularly if you're not completely attuned to how the recruiting game unfolds. No matter how well an athlete has performed in high school, or how hard he or she has prepared to compete at the next level, there are hurdles to negotiate to make the jump to a college campus.

In my case, I had all the proper credentials—I had lettered in four sports in high school, proven myself as a football running back for two years, was league champion in several track events (the 100, 220, and 4x100 relay), bench-pressed 380 pounds as a junior, and achieved good grades and SAT scores. During my junior year, I had received nearly seven hundred pieces of mail from the athletic departments of colleges and universities. As my senior season began, I figured I could almost choose from among the many colleges— including Notre Dame, the University of Southern California, and the University of California—that had expressed an interest in me (and a desire for a relationship with me), and had bombarded my home with phone calls, telegrams, personal notes, and promises.

But then reality hit hard in a number of unexpected ways. Early in my senior year, I tore ligaments in my left ankle, which forced me onto the bench for eight weeks of the football season. My high school coaches began treating me in ways that left me feeling isolated, and they questioned my toughness, commitment, and loyalty. At the same time, most college coaches stopped calling, thinking of me as damaged goods, although several did continue recruiting me. A few telegrams from colleges came trickling in, and I still clung to two solid offers, and two others that were possibilities, with those coaches encouraging me to get healthy quickly. They would say things like, "Once that ankle heals, we want you to be a part of our program."

One Monday night, I received a call from Ara Parseghian, then the head coach at Notre Dame. He informed me that he was resigning from the university, but said that he would recommend me to the new coaching staff; his assistant coach (Bill Hickey), who had actually done the hands-on recruiting of me, was expected to stay on board as part of the new coaching team.

Although I was disappointed by Parseghian's departure, I thought my dream was still alive. Shortly thereafter, Bob Lord, another Notre Dame assistant coach, invited me to attend the Notre Dame–USC football game at the Los Angeles Coliseum—right about the time my own high school basketball season was beginning. But my high school basketball coach refused to excuse me from a game of our own that afternoon so I could go to the Coliseum, insisting that my first commitment was to my team. (I ended up playing only four minutes in that high school game, although the coach had told me that the team was relying on my contribution that day.)

I was stunned and hurt by how little support I was getting at my own high school. I felt I had done everything that had been asked of me—and more. I had even remained loyal to my football coach when he challenged me during spring practice to choose between being a sprinter on the track team or a tailback on the football squad. However, as I recognized that the coach was doing nothing to promote me athletically, this experience actually gave me additional motivational "fuel" that helped get me where I wanted to be.

As the weeks passed and the recruiting process unfolded, most of the promises I had heard from college coaches turned out to be hollow. Nevertheless, I persevered, and ended up at a school—the University of California at Riverside—where I had the opportunity to grow up athletically, emotionally, and socially. UC Riverside was about as far removed as you can get from Notre Dame and the rich traditions of college football, and when I arrived there, my head was down and I was feeling rejected by the whole recruiting game. I quickly discovered, however, that I was playing alongside athletes who were every bit as talented as most Notre Damers. Many were transfers from UCLA, California, and numerous JCs that had won state titles. Butch Johnson was our senior wide receiver (he can still be seen on highlight films of the Super Bowls he starred in for the Dallas Cowboys and the Denver Broncos). My first college coach was Bob Toledo, now the head coach at UCLA, and he gave me the chance to play. My UC Riverside teammates helped me adjust my attitude toward Division II football (while also adjusting several of my vertebrae!). But I had also learned some hard lessons about how ruthless the recruiting process can be—and I vowed that if there were a way to help young athletes avoid some of the land mines that had exploded in my path, I would do so.

With that in mind, read on and incorporate the following information into the steps you take and the decisions you make. You and your family need to show diligence and skill in understanding, managing, and controlling the recruiting process. When you do, your own road to college will become a much less rocky one.

BECOMING PROACTIVE IN RECRUITING

The recruiting process can and should be exciting for students and their parents. When you begin getting attention from big and small colleges, it can be euphoric. Each time the phone rings with a call from a university coach and perhaps an offer of a trip to a college campus, your excitement level can understandably soar.

But don't let yourself become so intoxicated that you lose sight of exactly what is happening. From beginning to end, this is a process that you (and your parents) should control as much as possible with clear thinking and decision making. There *are* strategies for getting noticed by the schools that are most important to you, and to rise above the masses of other high school athletes, most of whom may ultimately get bypassed. However, you have to be willing to take charge of your own future.

WHERE DO YOU STAND?

So often in my current business, when I ask high school athletes where they think they stand in the recruiting game, I hear answers like, "I'm keeping all my options open," or "I'm not sure yet." These are the canned statements of players (and often their parents) who have no idea where they are in the process. Frequently, my response to them is, "What options are you keeping open?"—particularly when it's January 15 and they haven't received a call since September, and they have no tangible evidence of being recruited. While they may still have hopes and dreams, I'd have to say their options are closed!

It's important to understand as fully as possible the whirlwind of recruiting, and to take advantage of every opportunity. As you sort out where you stand in the race for college admissions and an athletic scholarship, keep this good news in mind: If you've really proven yourself, excelling in the classroom and on the athletic field in high school, you *will* get attention and you *will* be recruited. If you've achieved in a way that opens eyes, if you have the physical size that shows you can play at the college level, *and* if you have the grades and SAT scores to get you in the admissions door, then you really do have options, and it's very likely that you'll rise above the recruiting cattle call. I've described young athletes in this enviable position as "All dressed up and ready to go."

TIME FOR ANOTHER REALITY CHECK

Once again, refer back to the reality check in chapter 1. Throughout your high school years—but certainly no later than your junior year—you need to ask yourself questions like:

- Am I good enough to play in college?
- Do I have the physical skills to play collegiately?
- Do I really want to play at the next level?
- What have I achieved academically?

Make sure everything in the high school classroom is in order. Are you working hard to excel academically—particularly in your sophomore, junior, and senior years—thus ensuring that your grades won't slam any doors shut, and in fact will open many for you? A GPA of about 3.3 or better can dramatically broaden your windows of opportunity, compensating for any shortcomings you may have in other areas. As I've already noted, it will also attract the attention of universities with strict academic entrance requirements—like the Ivy League colleges, the service academies, Duke, Stanford, and Northwestern; with a high GPA, coupled with athletic achievement, these schools will *have* to take a hard look at you.

FINE-TUNING YOUR ATHLETIC SKILLS

On the athletic side, use the information in chapter 2 ("Improving Your Physical Prowess") to help you reach your physical peak. Even during the off-season, you should be on a training program that includes a refinement of your game. Stay focused on your goals so you'll be ready for the moment when the season officially begins, and college coaches are allowed to observe your games in person as part of the recruiting process. (In football, spring evaluations can occur during your junior year; your off-season preparation is important so that you make a good impression when college coaches get a look at you during the spring—and begin making their recruiting decisions.)

There is another important opportunity available to help you sharpen your athletic skills—and more. Every major university conducts summer camps for high school students in most sports. They're a money-making vehicle for the college, but just as significantly, they're a way for schools to bring young athletes to their campuses to evaluate and perhaps start recruiting some of them. At the same time, these camps can be a valuable learning experience for high school athletes, who will receive instruction from college-level coaches and get a sense of how the coaching staff interacts with young athletes. They'll also live in a dorm and catch a glimpse of what college life is all about. Later in this chapter, I'll discuss these camps in more detail.

HOW COLLEGES RECRUIT

As I've mentioned, college recruiting is a nonstop process. It's intense and competitive in both men's and women's sports. "There's always something we're working on, no matter what time of year it is," says David Tipton of Stanford University. "We're mailing out questionnaires, evaluating those that come in, compiling information from scouting services, making weekly phone calls once it's okay to do so, making home visits, and arranging for athletes to travel to our campus. Recruiting never stops."

During a recent recruiting season, the Stanford football program started out with the names of 4,000 possible recruits—and had twenty-one scholarships to award. "It's a constant process of evaluating and narrowing, evaluating and narrowing," says Tipton.

THE DIVISION OF RESPONSIBILITIES

In every college sport, head coaches and their assistants divide the recruiting responsibilities among themselves. Here is how the hierarchy is structured:

The head coach typically oversees the recruiting process, but appoints one of his assistants as recruiting coordinator. Other assistant coaches will play important roles in recruiting as well (although their numbers vary from school to school, and from sport to sport).

Colleges that recruit nationally divide the country into regions, and each assistant coach is assigned a geographical area for which he or she is responsible. Other colleges, particularly those with small recruiting budgets and/or high out-of-state tuition, limit their recruiting to their own region or state (and they may utilize a general recruiting office in the athletic department that responds to mail and oversees a lot of the other recruiting paperwork). No matter what the scenario, every coach must take an NCAA-administered test every year, confirming his or her understanding of the rules and regulations of recruiting. (The test really isn't very rigorous, particularly since it is an open book exam!)

WHAT ARE A COLLEGE'S OWN ATHLETIC NEEDS?

As each sport's season ends, the next recruiting year begins. Thus, when the basketball season winds up in March, or the baseball season finishes in May, the respective college coaching staffs begin concentrating on recruiting, creating their priority lists of the types of players they need to recruit, based on the projected team roster for the following year(s). Coaches will evaluate their immediate needs, including the number of scholarships available for the upcoming academic year (the NCAA mandates how many scholarships can be granted in each sport). In coaches' meetings, they'll ask themselves questions like, "Who are we losing due to graduation, academic ineligibility, or injuries? How many slots do we have to fill? Who might be granted red-shirt status? What type of players do we need to bring in? What are our immediate needs? What positions do we need to make priorities?"

Immediate needs may arise due to foreseen and unforeseen events. For example, there may have been "mistakes" in last year's recruiting class, and new talent must be found to fill the positions of players who didn't work out as planned. Many athletes live up to expectations, but others simply don't.

Thus, long before they formally put the recruiting bait in the water, coaches know what kind of fish they want, the depth of the water, and exactly what they have to do to get the strike. In volleyball, for example, the coaches may decide they need to recruit a middle blocker and an outside hitter this year. In baseball, the coaches' "wish list" might include a left-handed pitcher, a power-hitting third baseman, and a catcher. So if you're a left fielder, you might not get much attention from those coaches, simply because they're already well stocked with players at your position.

In a sport like football, of course, where team rosters are much larger than in other sports, the national powers recruit so deep that their first two (and perhaps even third) units could play anywhere in the country. Well-established programs are looking for recruits who are going to help them three, four, and even five years down the road. Players who become starters as "true freshmen" (their first year out of high school) have usually demonstrated talent far above and beyond their peer group. These players possess so many athletic skills, and so much poise and physical maturity, that they can be placed in a starting role immediately.

Whenever you see a true freshman starting, you are watching a truly gifted athlete. In general, however, true freshmen starters are rare. College coaches must prioritize their recruiting, often looking to the junior colleges to meet their immediate needs, and to the high schools for players who may develop into starters within two to three years.

THE ROLE OF NOTE CARDS

A college's recruiting coordinator is responsible for disseminating recruiting materials to high schools and junior colleges early in the process. Most colleges distribute three-by-five-inch note cards to all the high school and junior college coaches in their recruiting areas, asking them to list the top talent at their school, along with some brief biographical information about each of these student-athletes, including height, weight, speed, and an estimated GPA. This request for information may also ask each coach to list the top players in the league, section, and county. These cards are generally distributed in February and March of each year, although the time may vary depending on the sport.

When the cards are returned to the athletic department, they become sources of leads and a means of cross-checking talent and information. The recruiting coordinator collects, sorts, and reviews these cards and passes them along to the coaches overseeing each region. The assistant coaches then place their prospects into categories; if they are not already familiar with a particular young athlete, they may make phone calls to confirm certain information (including size, speed, and GPA).

WHAT DO QUESTIONNAIRES MEAN?

The university will usually send out a letter and a questionnaire to each identified potential recruit (see page 84 for a sample questionnaire). Many major college football programs mail out these questionnaires to four hundred to five hundred young athletes a year as part of their canvassing process. As exciting as it may be to receive mail from universities and their coaches, don't overestimate its significance. Student-athletes often read these letters and exclaim, "Wow, I'm being recruited by Notre Dame (or Cal or Nebraska)." But that couldn't be further from the truth.

Quite frankly, at this stage, it's all just mail. You might think you're being recruited, but the college coaches are thinking, "We're still canvassing." It's only a way for them to gather information in the early stages of recruiting. At some colleges, their computer mailing lists are updated so infrequently that form letters may be sent out routinely to high school students in whom interest has long since waned. (One of my players is still receiving mail at home from a university two years after his own recruiting process was completed; yes, recruiting can be an inexact science!)

OTHER SOURCES OF INFORMATION

Independent scouting services may also be providing college coaches with data about the backgrounds of athletes in particular regions. Representatives of these services talk with high school coaches, identify top talent at each school, and provide this information to colleges. As well as offering the cosmetic numbers (height, weight, etc.), they may also conduct player evaluations by attending games and practices. Then there are the independent video services, which shoot videotapes of top candidates and distribute them to colleges that may request them. All this information will eventually have to be either validated or discarded, but it goes into the files of college coaches to help them in the sifting and sorting process.

Depending on the sport, college coaches have still other avenues for finding top recruits. Swimming coaches, for instance, routinely attend national championship swim meets to watch high school–age athletes compete. "We follow fifteen- and sixteen-year-old swimmers for a couple years, observe whether they're getting better, whether their mechanics are improving, and whether they've been working to stay in top physical condition so they can compete at the Division I level," says Terri McKeever, women's swimming coach at the University of California at Berkeley.

At the same time, college coaches like McKeever are talking to club coaches (as well as high school coaches) about particular swimmers. "We've developed relationships with these coaches," she says. "We trust what they say, not only about their own swimmers but also about other swimmers in their area. We rely a lot on these networks that we've built up."

CONSOLIDATING THE RAW DATA

Over the ensuing weeks and months, coaches will continue to accumulate, consolidate, and refine their raw data. They may request transcripts and additional videos. They will make phone calls to the recruits themselves and their families (within NCAA guidelines), and they will attend high school games. They often turn again to their coaching colleagues to gain insights into particular athletes and to confirm information.

Before a college coach ever "hits the recruiting trail," traveling to high school campuses or making home visits, he may have weighed and evaluated information on literally thousands of prospects. A major college football program may begin with a preliminary list of 2,500 to 4,000 athletes. Over time, this number will be reduced to 500 prospects, which includes an elite 100. This list of the "Super 100" is composed of student-athletes who could go to any college in the country, and for that reason, those additional 400 names are kept as an important backup—readily available if coaches need to fall back to the second tier of possible recruits.

WHAT ABOUT ONE-ON-ONE CONTACTS?

During the initial stages of recruiting, while coaches are creating their priorities and collecting information on athletes, one element is glaringly absent—namely, personal contact between the high school player and the college coach. Aside from the relatively innocuous questionnaire, the colleges cannot mail any letters to a player until September 1 at the beginning of the young person's junior year. The first phone contact cannot occur until the summer before the student's senior year. In chapter 7, I'll go into more detail about these NCAA rules and restrictions on when a college coach may legally write and call you. However, as you'll discover in the next chapter, these restrictions do *not* prevent you or your parents from making appropriate calls yourselves to coaches—but more about that later.

When a coach hits the road to meet with athletes and to observe talent, one of his goals is to find out from the prospects themselves (and their parents) about the schools in which they're most interested. In the race toward signing day, coaches are trying to secure commitments from athletes to visit their campuses as early in the process as possible.

CAN MISTAKES BE AVOIDED?

Good coaches try to avoid putting themselves in a position of disqualifying talent in a manner that could come back to haunt them. They're constantly double-checking and triple-checking information on prospects, and tracking who their competitors at other colleges are looking at and considering. Before eliminating any candidate from the process, they'll move a step back and take another hard look at the prospect, trying to cut down on human error as much as possible (although because the system is managed by people, mistakes are inevitable).

THE COLLEGE QUESTIONNAIRE

You may receive a questionnaire like the one below from the athletic departments of one or more colleges. These questionnaires may be sports-specific, or they can be more general in nature. As you can see, you will probably be asked to provide data about your height, weight, and running speed. It will also request personal information such as your parents' occupations, the names and ages of your brothers and sisters, your hobbies, career goals, and GPA. You might also be asked about your religion, your favorite player(s), the names of colleges you'd like to attend, and some sports-specific information similar to what appears in the following sample. The letter may also request an unofficial transcript of your high school grades, and, of course, your home phone number. By all means, fill out the questionnaire and return it, but don't make more of it than it really warrants.

Also, provide accurate information, whether on these questionnaires or in any other format in which it may be offered. "One of the first things we do is verify the information a student gives us," says coach David Tipton of Stanford. "We'll call the student's high school counselor to confirm his grades. Sometimes, the student who has written down a GPA of 3.4 will have only a 2.4." And at universities like Stanford, which put a strong emphasis on academics, a 2.4 GPA is going to force coaches to look at a candidate much differently.

Student-Athlete Questionnaire

Full name: _____ Nickname: _____

Address: _____

City: _____ State: _____ Zip Code: _____

Home phone: _____ Parent's work phone: _____

Date of birth: _____ Social Security #: _____

Father's name: _____ Occupation: _____

Mother's name: _____ Occupation: _____

Brothers/sisters (& ages): _____

Colleges attended by parents/siblings: _____

Are you married? _____ Religion (optional): _____

Your high school: _____

Your sport(s): _____

Position(s): _____ Left- or right-handed: _____

Your high school coach(es): _____

Your height: _____ weight: _____

Statistics in your sport (e.g., batting average, points scored,
    tackles, etc.): _____

Speed: 10 yd ____ 30 yd _____ 40 yd ____ 60 yd _____
    100 yd _____ 120 yd ____

Bench press: total reps @ 225 lb ____ @ 185 lb _____
    @ 135 lb _____

3/4 squat: total reps @ 225 lb _____ @ 185 lb _____
    @ 135 lb _____

GPA: _____ Expected date of graduation: _____

Favorite classes: _____

Career goals: _____

PSAT score: _____ SAT score: _____ ACT score: _____

If you haven't taken the SAT or ACT, when will you do so?

_____

Academic honors: _____

Athletic honors: _____

Hobbies: _____

Top 5 college choices: 1 _____ 2 _____
    3 _____ 4 _____ 5 _____

Favorite players: _____

Athletes/alumni you know at our college: _____

Have you registered with the NCAA's Initial Eligibility
    Clearinghouse? _____ If not, when do you plan to do
    so? _____

Will you send us an unofficial copy of your high school
    academic transcript? _____

Your signature: _____ Date: _____

THE VALUE OF A PERSONAL ASSESSMENT

The most efficient college recruiting programs begin tracking young athletes in their freshman and sophomore years of high school, occasionally even in junior high. But remember, the NCAA has specific guidelines on periods when college coaches can evaluate potential recruits, and how many such evaluations they can make. These coaches may visit high school campuses, where they can talk with counselors, principals, and coaches, as well as watch the athlete himself during practice—but only when recruiting rules allow them to do so.

Personally, when I was coaching, I could hardly wait to see the potential recruits in my area—not only watching them perform in game situations, but getting a sense of how they relate to teammates during practices, their work ethic, and all the other intangible qualities. Is he the first person on the field and the last one off? Is he a team player? How does he compare to the other candidates I'm keeping an eye on?

I also believed it was important to observe and evaluate a young athlete's character. Sure, assessing character is subjective, but I could get a sense of it by watching each potential recruit interact with his peers and coaches. Was this candidate acting the role of "big-time Charlie," or was he a genuine person? I knew a few of these seventeen- and eighteen-year-olds would be millionaires in four to five years, but even so, it was important for them to have their feet on the ground and their egos under control. Junior Seau was one of those athletes. Years before he became an NFL all-star with the San Diego Chargers, he had it all in terms of both character and talent. I remember visiting him at his high school and at his home, and knowing that this young man would have a positive impact on everyone he met.

WHAT CAN YOUR HIGH SCHOOL COACH DO?

Although your own high school coach is probably in touch with many college coaches, you can't rely on him or her to help you squeeze a foot in the door at the schools in which you're interested. One of the most frequent complaints I hear from student-athletes is,

"My coach isn't doing anything for me!" But don't create unrealistic expectations. Many high school coaches are so overwhelmed with just keeping their own sports programs functioning that they have little or no time to run interference for you, other than jotting down your name and personal information on a three-by-five card. And after all, where does it say in their job description that their role is to do anything more than be a teacher and a coach?

Of course, you want your coach to be your ally if he or she is asked about your talent and abilities. But your coach can't get you a scholarship (although some may say they can). Ultimately, *you* and *your* efforts will get you everything you're capable of achieving.

Remember, if a high school coach really goes out on a limb for one of his players, it could even cost him his good standing with his peers, particularly if his praise seems overstated. Also, high school coaches (like most of the rest of us) are looking out for their own careers, and *their* best interest may not also coincide with *yours*. Some may *undervalue* a player to preserve their relationship with a college coach, just as others may *exaggerate* their player's talents, hoping to attract the attention of colleges to their own high school program. The latter may work one time, but it can damage the reciprocal trust between high school and college coaches.

Of course, depending on the passion you show on and off the athletic field, your high school coach just might end up telling the college recruiter, "I can only say that this kid has played great for me, and is the hardest worker in my program. She's loyal, and she hasn't missed a practice in three years. It's attitudes like hers that have made us a winning team. And she's doing very well academically, too." You couldn't ask for anything more.

Let me also say, however, that I find it offensive for a college coach to specifically ask a high school (or junior college) coach whether a particular athlete can compete at the next level. Yes, the player may have performed for that high school coach throughout the entire season in an exemplary manner; even so, the coach may have never played or worked with athletes at the college level. Thus, when I was coaching at Stanford and San Jose State, even though I took the coach's comments into consideration if he offered them, I never thought of it as the final word.

JUDGING A COLLEGE'S RECRUITING PROGRAM

From the college's point of view, recruiting is hard, painstaking work. A coach's longevity at a particular college depends in part on his or her success in recruiting. The process is not approached cavalierly, since coaches know that their recruiting today will translate into wins or losses for their program in the years ahead. Students and their parents should judge a college program by the sincerity, passion, and professional manner in which it conducts its recruiting.

By the way, in this chapter, I'm describing recruiting as it *should* be done by college coaches, and the meticulous manner in which it is conducted by the best of them. Great programs, for example, are already thinking about the *next* recruiting season while this one is still ongoing. Unfortunately, however, too many colleges adopt a "fire-aim-ready" approach to recruiting. They are very unorganized, and thus waste lots of time chasing recruits who are unattainable, and neglecting some whom they should be pursuing. Too many coaches are driven by the attitude, "I can't be bothered with recruiting until this season is over." They've become accustomed to letting other colleges recruit, and then knocking on the doors of those athletes who have been bypassed and "discarded." It is a haphazard approach to recruiting and a clear indication that a program is in trouble.

CAN PRIVATE RECRUITING SERVICES HELP?

Most parents and students know very little about college recruiting when the process begins, and thus they may turn to a private recruiting service or marketing service for help. They might attend a seminar or read a brochure, which promises to market their youngster to hundreds of college athletic departments. For a hefty fee (usually several hundred dollars), some of these commercial services all but "guarantee" admission to a major college and a sports scholarship. Frankly, many are very good at selling anxiety, convincing parents that they "need" this service to keep their child from being trampled in the stampede toward a college scholarship.

These services generally prepare a mass mailing—a one- or two-page description of each athlete along with a photo—sent to perhaps

1,500 colleges, which will produce 1,500 form responses from college athletic departments. This deluge of return mail convinces many students (and their parents) that they're being actively recruited. But it really doesn't mean much at all—and it may actually be counterproductive.

FLOODING THE COACHES' DESKS

The megamarketing mentality that floods college athletic departments with résumés and sometimes videotapes—many promoting students who do not fit a particular college's profile—can leave coaches frustrated and overwhelmed. (Imagine receiving 100 pieces of unsolicited mail per week—most of them form letters and Xerox copies of résumés—that, in a sense, are telling you how to do your job.)

"Remember that in football and basketball, college recruiting is coming down to a science," says Andy Bark, publisher of *Student Sports Magazine*. "Coaches attend combines, they rely on their own recruiting services, and they have huge budgets for going out and looking at the prospects personally. So are they going to look at a Xerox photocopy that comes in from a commercial service? No. They've already bought fifteen lists, and merged and purged them. Or they've done eyeball evaluations of their own."

However, in the nonrevenue-producing sports with limited recruiting budgets, coaches may be more eager for information, adds Bark. But even then, he says, some college coaches may think, "If the student has paid six hundred dollars for a private recruiting service, why didn't she use that same money to play club volleyball instead, where she could really show off her talents?"

HOW LEGITIMATE ARE THESE SERVICES?

Some of these businesses have begun to promote the names of players who have used their services—in violation of NCAA rules that prohibit the names of athletes with current eligibility from being included in marketing efforts. (I wonder how one of these so-called scholarship hunters will react when they are responsible for their "prospects" losing their eligibility.)

Some of my present clients had once signed up with these services, only to find that the people who run them didn't even know some of the simplest pieces of information, such as when recruiting season begins from the college's perspective. In one case, a former major league baseball star, Doug DeCinces, was told that a scholarship was available for his son, Tim—but he had to sign up for the service to get it! That's ridiculous. Tim got the scholarship on his own. He played baseball at UCLA, was invited to the U.S. Olympics baseball tryouts in 1995 and was drafted by the Baltimore Orioles in 1996.

GET IT IN WRITING

If these services still offer something that interests you, get in writing what they're going to provide. Also, ask for written answers to questions like these: "Who are your past and present clients? . . . What colleges have they been admitted to? . . . What scholarships did they receive?" You might be surprised by the answers and decide not to spend the money after all.

Andy Bark says, "These recruiting services are catching desperate parents who look at the financial realities of college, and are told, 'You make a $600 investment now, and it will mean a $60,000 scholarship.' Any economist will tell you that's a great investment; unfortunately, it's not a sure thing."

Ironically, many players with whom I speak are very realistic about where they can and cannot play; form letters from major colleges flatter their parents but create an unrealistic expectation about the young person's future.

CAN YOU DO IT YOURSELF INSTEAD?

The bottom line is that most of these services are an expensive exercise in futility. On your own, you can accomplish most or all of what these information brokers can, and do it in a much more personal way and for much less money. Remember, college coaches want to know if a particular boy or girl can play his or her sport, and if he or she is genuinely interested in their college; the fancy stationery and the mass mailings to hundreds of schools isn't going to impress very many—if any—college coaches.

Finally, keep in mind that even though many people claim to be college scouts (often in violation of NCAA rules), the only individuals who can really represent and recruit for a school are its coaches. By talking to anyone else, you are probably just wasting your time and increasing your vulnerability.

CONFIRMING YOUR ELIGIBILITY

If you have your eyes set on playing at a Division I or II college as a freshman, you *must* register with the NCAA Initial-Eligibility Clearinghouse. By submitting the proper documents to the clearinghouse, the NCAA can certify that you have met the criteria and are eligible to compete at the college level. It will *not* help you gain admittance to a college or earn a scholarship; but it will let colleges know that you have attained the eligibility requirements in terms of your GPA and SAT/ACT scores.

The best place to start this eligibility process is right at your own high school, where your guidance counselor should have the NCAA registration (or student-release) forms you need to fill out and submit. (If he or she doesn't have these forms, they can be obtained from the NCAA clearinghouse by calling (319) 337-1492.) Your counselor should also be able to provide you with a brochure called, "Making Sure You Are Eligible to Participate in College Sports."

The best time to submit the clearinghouse form is once your grades in your high school junior year become part of your transcript. (The earlier the form is submitted, the better your chances of detecting and then resubmitting the occasional lost forms and resolving other problems that have surrounded the clearinghouse.) Mail the white copy to the clearinghouse address listed on the document. Be sure to include the registration fee (which was eighteen dollars at the time of this writing, although a waiver of the fee is sometimes possible). Then, give the yellow and pink copies of the form to your high school counselor, who will keep the pink copy in the school's own files and send the yellow copy to the clearinghouse, accompanied by your official high school transcript. (At the end of your senior year, your counselor must submit a copy of your final transcript to the clearinghouse, confirming that you have graduated.)

Your SAT or ACT scores must also be sent to the clearinghouse. The testing agency itself should submit your scores directly. (The SAT and ACT registration forms have a place to indicate that you want your scores mailed to the clearinghouse; specifically, look for and mark "code 9999.") Your test scores can also be reported as part of your official high school transcript.

Once your name and other information are on file with the NCAA, colleges that may be interested in you will contact the clearinghouse to ensure that you have met the eligibility criteria.

CHAPTER 6

CREATING A GAME PLAN

As I've written repeatedly, it's important for you and your parents to take charge of your own college recruiting. That means not waiting for the colleges to make the first move, because in many cases, it will never happen. Instead, position yourself so you and your family are in control of the process. Long before coaches can legally make contact with you, you and your family can send a letter and other materials that are much more meaningful than filling out a questionnaire and may prompt a more substantial response.

MAKING A LIST OF COLLEGES

To get started, while you're actively working on your physical development and academics in high school, it's also time to make a list of the colleges you'd like to attend. In your junior year of high school (or earlier if you wish), sit down as a family, and list twenty colleges to whom you would like to introduce yourself, and let them know of your interest in their academic and sports programs. Rather than taking a shotgun approach of contacting dozens and dozens of schools, pare your list down to twenty. Actually, you might have to stretch a little to get to even twenty; most students run out of names after five or six, and grab the sports section of the newspaper for help, or look at the television listings to see who's playing on TV on Saturday. So it might be a struggle to get to twenty, but come as close as possible.

More than anything, make sure you've filled your list with the names of schools you'd like to attend and graduate from, and colleges that offer a program in your expected academic major; if that same college also has a team in your sport, you have the best of all worlds. Your high school guidance counselor should have current reference books and college catalogs in his or her office that will help you find out about the sports and academic departments in the colleges you're considering.

In your list of twenty, include a few dream schools—perhaps UCLA, the University of Michigan, or Florida State. If you've done very well academically, add one or more of the service academies (Navy, Army, Air Force), and a couple of the Ivy League schools like Princeton, Harvard, or Dartmouth. As a start, use the list of colleges in the appendix of this book, but also spend an hour doing research at the resource center of your high school, and choose not only some Division I-A colleges but also some Division I-AAs, IIs, IIIs, and NAIAs.

WHAT DO DIVISION DESIGNATIONS MEAN?

As of the 1996–97 school year, the NCAA had classified 305 colleges as Division I, 246 as Division II, and 352 as Division III. (In football, Division I is further divided into Division I-A and I-AA.) Most high school athletes probably dream of playing at the Division I level in front of packed stadiums and large TV audiences. But there's not enough room for everyone at Division I, and the level of play in Divisions II and III is very competitive. Even more important, some of the nation's finest *academic* institutions have athletic programs that are in Division II or III.

Schools at the Divisions II and III levels are often smaller colleges. However, a college becomes categorized as Division I, II, or III not by the size of its student body or the success of its athletic program but by factors such as the seating capacity of its football stadium. If thirty thousand or more fans can fit into the football stadium, or if the college has averaged more than seventeen thousand in paid attendance per home football game over the previous four years, then it meets the criteria of Division I-A; smaller football seating capacities or attendance earn the school status in another division.

The divisions also differ in the number of athletic scholarships they can offer. Take football, for example: In 1996, a Division I college could award eighty-five football scholarships; at Division II, the limit was thirty-six; and at Division III, no scholarships were available. But keep in mind that at Division II, even though there are fewer scholarships, coaches usually become quite creative in breaking up the available money into partial scholarships—half rides, quarter rides, and so on—so that more student-athletes receive at least some financial help for the skyrocketing cost of a college education.

CRITERIA FOR YOUR COLLEGE LIST

When you're making the list of colleges you'd like to attend, there are a number of factors to keep in mind. Of course, you want to know if they have an active intercollegiate program in your sport. But there are many other considerations, too. Here are some questions to get answered, either from reference books in your high school resource center, or from coaches and/or admissions-office representatives of each college you're considering:

- Does the college offer a major in my particular area of academic interest? Does the school have a good overall academic reputation?
- Are the classes in my major offered only at times that will conflict with my sport in any way?
- What is the graduation rate for student-athletes at the college? How does that compare with the graduation rate for nonathletes? (The NCAA prepares Graduation-Rates Reports on America's colleges, based on information provided by these institutions; each Division I and II college is required to make this report available to prospective student-athletes.)
- Is the college large or small? Would I prefer to attend a school with a large student body (and larger class sizes), or a smaller college where I might fit in more quickly and be able to have more frequent interactions with my professors? What is the student-faculty ratio at the college?
- Is the college coeducational, or is it only (or primarily) a men's or a women's school? Which do I prefer?
- Are there other opportunities available for my nonacademic interests—perhaps an active music department or clubs that cater to the type of recreation I enjoy (like a skiing or a mountain-climbing club)?

- If I do not earn a full-ride athletic scholarship, are the tuition and other costs of the college affordable for me and my family? Am I willing to take out student loans for my costs not covered by an athletic scholarship?
- Is student housing easily available and affordable?
- Is the college so far away that it will be costly for me to visit home frequently—and expensive to call home? Would I become homesick being so far from home?
- Is the college in a small town or a big city? What size community would I be most comfortable living in?
- What's the weather like in the area? Can I adapt easily to temperatures and conditions that might be much warmer or colder (more rainy, snowy) than I'm used to?

WHAT ABOUT A VIDEO?

At the same time you're making your list of twenty colleges, begin thinking of putting together a brief videotape that you can use to show college coaches your athletic abilities. Videos don't lie; they'll demonstrate just how good you are, no matter how much (or how little) media coverage you got and regardless of whether you were ever named to the all-league team. The videotape doesn't have to be a Cecil B. DeMille production. Your mom or dad can use your family's video camera to tape you in action, but most high schools have video equipment, and their athletic events are taped for their own analysis and teaching purposes. Generally, you'll have access to these videotapes, and for a nominal cost, you can have sections of them copied and placed on a single tape, giving college coaches a glimpse of your abilities.

I consider the ideal tape a "teaser," lasting just three to six minutes and incorporating perhaps fifteen to twenty-five plays, hopefully enough to whet the appetite of the college coach who watches it. I'd also suggest adding a narration to the video, or sending a written script along with it, describing what's about to be shown. For example, the following entries are from the scripts prepared by three athletes—two of them football players and the third a basketball player:

Script 1: My uniform number on this videotape is 56, and there are 25 plays on it. Play #1: 97-yard kickoff return vs. Central High School; I'm outrunning number 33 in the green jersey, who was the state sprint champ in 1995 (10.6 100m).

Script 2: Play #5: Inside trap vs. Southern High School, in which I'm running by a linebacker (number 55) who is now a starter at Michigan.

Script 3: Play #8: Playing defense, I am pressuring and stealing the basketball from number 6 in the white jersey; he was an all-state point guard now playing at Georgetown.

Again, the video doesn't have to be elaborate or fancy. But it is an extremely effective promotional tool. Its intent is to validate your talents.

MAKING CONTACT WITH THE COLLEGES

Once you have completed your list of twenty colleges, and have the videotape in hand, it's time to begin cultivating a relationship with the coaches at these schools. After your sports season ends in your junior year of high school (in November, for example, if you play football; or in May if you play baseball), you (or a parent) should call the athletic departments of the twenty schools and confirm that your sport is offered there. (If you're calling a high-profile college, and you play a high-profile sport like football or basketball, you probably already know the answer.) Then request the name of the assistant coach for your sport who recruits in your part of the country, and an address where you can write to him or her. (You'll find many college addresses and phone numbers in the appendix of this book.) It's important to send these letters to a specific individual, rather than to "Dear Coach."

Next, write letters to each of these coaches. Although college coaches themselves are restricted in the contacts they can initiate, you have no such restrictions. So you and your parents should compose a letter of introduction, letting each coach know that you exist, that you're interested in attending his or her college, and what you've accomplished academically and athletically thus far in high school. If you were a starter on your team during the past season, be sure to mention that in the letter. If you were named "Player of the Week" by a local newspaper, or if you won a scholar-athlete award or were named all-league, include that as well. If you're proud of your GPA, mention it.

This initial letter of introduction should be written and signed by your parent, ideally your father; in a single-parent home, or one in which there is a legal guardian, the head of the home should sign the letter. The power of this letter written by your "overseer" is essential in setting the right tone for recruiting. It demonstrates that an adult is directing the process, and that your parent values his or her child as the most prized possession within the home.

If possible, type the letter, or write it on a computer. Handwritten letters are fine, too, as long as the penmanship is neat and legible. Check for and eliminate spelling and grammar errors before sealing the envelope and placing it in the mailbox.

The following sample letter gives the college coach information that would normally take weeks for him or her to gather. Make sure this information is accurate.

SAMPLE LETTER TO COLLEGE COACH

Dear Coach Sample:

My name is Jim Walsh, and I am writing to you on behalf of my daughter, Kylee. She is currently a junior at Leland High School in San Jose, California. I have enclosed an unofficial transcript that shows her 3.65 GPA in her core classes. Kylee has taken the SAT and scored a combined 1150, with a math score of 600 and a verbal score of 550. She was recently elected student body treasurer, and is very active in community service programs for the elderly.

Kylee is a 5'8", 135-pound point guard, and will be a starter for the third year this season. She was named CIF (California Interscholastic Federation) Girls' Basketball Player of the Year last season, as well as All-State, All-League, and her team's

Most Valuable Player. This past year, she averaged 25 points, 12 assists, 4 rebounds and 6 steals per game.

Kylee attended the basketball camp at Cal Berkeley last summer, and I have enclosed her evaluation. I am also sending along a brief video of Kylee in game situations that demonstrates her skills offensively and defensively.

Kylee is interested in attending another basketball camp next summer, and we would like to obtain more information about yours. Our home address is 22333 Main Street, San Jose, California 99999. Our home phone number is (408) 555-1222, and my work number is (408) 555-2333. We look forward to hearing from you.

Sincerely,

James K. Walsh

WHAT IMPACT DOES THE LETTER HAVE?

The letter above achieves something that most letters don't: It includes important elements that set it apart from the majority of letters that arrive at the athletic office. First, the academic transcript is crucial (although it is something that students usually fail to enclose), as are the SAT scores. Since many coaches rank high school athletes by their grades, test scores, and honors, this information is an invaluable part of the process, and gives them something they can begin to evaluate. Your SAT or ACT scores are often part of your transcript, but if not, make a photocopy of your test results and include it with the letter. With that kind of documentation in hand, the coach will often react by thinking, "Her grades and test scores look very good; by our college's academic guidelines, she is someone I can recruit. I'll watch the videotape her father sent and see if she can play." In minutes, an unknown athlete can become someone in whom the coach begins showing interest.

Nearly every letter that arrives on a coach's desk will generate at least a form-letter response, often addressed to "Dear Prospective Athlete," along with a questionnaire. Your incoming letter will become part of the coach's files, and he or she may begin to track you. When I was recruiting at Stanford, I had a so-called active file, which included high school players I wanted to make sure I kept tabs on. Many of these young student-athletes got into that file through unsolicited letters they had written to me.

As the sample letter indicates, send a copy of your videotape along with the letter. By mentioning in the letter that the tape is only a few minutes long, the coach will know that it's not going to take much of her time to review it—so she probably will take a look. You are asking the college coach for three to six minutes of time—and after viewing the video, you want her to react by asking for more!

As part of the packet you're mailing to college coaches, consider sending letters of recommendation from your high school coach or club team coach, if you're confident they have real value—for example, a recommendation letter could come from a high school coach who has a lineage of players who have excelled at the college level. These letters may describe your athletic talents and accomplishments, and your personal characteristics and qualities. Letters from teachers, counselors, and principals can also help create a character and academic profile. A camp evaluation would offer another independent view of your athletic abilities.

WHAT ABOUT SUMMER CAMP?

When you send those letters and videos to the college coaches you've chosen, mention that you may be interested in signing up for their college camp in your particular sport (if they have one). See the sample letter on pages 98–99, or insert a few sentences such as:

> I plan to attend a baseball camp this summer.
> Does your university offer a camp? If so, please
> send me a brochure about it.

Most coaches will not ignore a potential camper. Your attendance means revenue (an average of $400 to $600) and an evaluation that may give them a unique advantage during recruiting. So you'll win some instant leverage with him or her. Within a week or two, you will probably get a personal letter, a brochure, and perhaps even a phone call (depending on whether that call conflicts with NCAA rules). I think it's valuable for you to attend one or more of these camps. They can be a wonderful showcase for your talents in front of the coaches who are the ultimate decision makers in the awarding of scholarships. You'll be playing your sport at these week-long camps, and not only will coaches be assessing your athletic abilities, they'll be judging your attitude and work ethic as well.

There's an important caveat, however: Yes, you're going to camp for reasons beyond just displaying your abilities and moving a step closer to a scholarship; after all, it will be a fun and enjoyable week, where you can get a sense of where you fit in with other athletes in your sport. Even so, think twice about attending a camp if you're not physically ready to perform at your peak. A three-sport athlete, for example, may have spent the last several months playing baseball and thus hasn't thrown or caught a football in that long; he'd be doing himself a disservice by signing up for a football camp. If you haven't been training in your sport, and your skills aren't as finely tuned as they could be, you might sabotage your dreams at a camp —and throw away some money in the process.

If you're in peak form, however, a camp will give you a sense of where you stand among your peers, and it could catapult you to the top of the list of high school recruits. Did you excel as the best three-point shooter at the camp? Did you perform better than the other quarterbacks there? Were you given a written evaluation from the college coach that validated your talents ("You're a recruitable athlete, and you're going to have a great college career")? Kind words, of course, aren't guarantees that you're going to be offered anything. But they can give your self-confidence a boost, and perhaps open some doors for you. Remember, character counts, and this is a great vehicle to show them what you're made of!

USING A CAMP TO FULL ADVANTAGE

Not long ago, I worked with a high school volleyball player named Omar Rawi, who was a good player with the right cosmetic features (6'5", 190 pounds). Even so, to insure that he had as impressive a physical presence as possible, I prepared a personalized training program for Omar. It included weight training, running drills, and, most important, court-related work. He arranged pickup games at the beach against top competition. I challenged him to look at his performance as a coach would, and he began to see that he could make unique contributions to a college team, and that he had genuine value in the college marketplace.

As Omar matured as an athlete, he began to dominate the volleyball court. He became a more aggressive, more confident player. His GPA was always solid, but he challenged himself with honors courses and set his sights even higher in the classroom. Omar was taking his game—and his life—A STEP BEYOND.

When Omar felt he was ready, he attended volleyball camps at both Stanford University and the University of California at Santa Barbara. And he couldn't have been better prepared. He went there to put on a performance that turned heads—and he did. He was six months ahead of most of his peers in terms of physical development and his ability to play his sport.

Volleyball camps are run differently than the camps of most other sports, in that coaches from other colleges can attend them at the host school and observe and evaluate the young athletes (although they can't approach or talk to them). At those camps, Omar's stock among college coaches soared. He won the most valuable player award at both camps. The most frequent comments from coaches were, "He's the hardest working kid here. . . . He has a wonderful attitude. . . . He's a dominant player. . . . He has great concentration."

After the camps, Omar was courted by many colleges, including some he had once believed he could attend only because of his academic prowess. But now he had become a recruitable *student-athlete*. I advised him not to eliminate any colleges yet. "You were named the camp's most valuable player, and you have a value now in their eyes," I told him. Omar began to enjoy the recruiting process, and he eventually signed a letter of intent to attend the University of Southern California, where he began his academic and athletic careers in the fall of 1995.

Would Omar have gotten noticed by colleges without the camps? Certainly. But he wouldn't have achieved the level of attention he did, nor would his impressive work ethic have been so obvious to so many coaches. Perhaps most important, Omar left the camps knowing how good he was. At those camps, he competed against other players whom he had once believed were better than him—and he outperformed them. At a camp, you have the opportunity to present yourself in the most favorable light possible—and Omar did just that.

CHOOSING A CAMP

So which camp should you select? All football (baseball, basketball, etc.) camps tend to be held during the same week—nearly every football camp, for example, is scheduled during the last week of June, while baseball camps are held in mid-August (as well as during Christmas break). So you'll have to choose among them. If finances are a concern, look for a day camp (rather than an overnight one), which will be less expensive because you won't be paying for room and board. Also, if you select a camp at a nearby college, you can avoid the cost of an airplane ticket.

If you can afford it, however, choose an overnight camp. In those four to five days, you'll get a real flavor of college and dorm life, as well as have more time to interact with the coaches on both a formal and informal basis. Camps are a time when coaches can get to know you as a player and as a person, and to measure your talents against other young athletes.

Look over the camp brochures that are sent to you, get a sense of which coaches (in addition to the head coach) will be running the camp, and whether there will be any guest speakers or coaches (former players from that college, pro players, Olympic-level athletes). Don't hesitate to ask questions and inquire about whether you'll receive an evaluation at the end of the week and from whom. (Obviously, you want something more constructive to take home with you than a camp T-shirt, a photo with the head coach, and the good-bye greeting, "Thanks, and we'll see you next time.")

In making your final decision, choose the camp where you feel you'll have the best overall experience. Don't get trapped into thinking, "I'm going to this camp because I want a scholarship from there!" After all, there are no guarantees of that, even though some of my players have performed so well at a camp that the coaches there began recruiting them. If you have the time and the finances to attend a camp—and you're ready to excel and demonstrate your strong work ethic—try to fit one into your summer schedule.

THE "COMBINE" ALTERNATIVE

There is another type of camplike event in which you may be able to participate. Since 1993, I have helped run one-day football "combines" in cooperation with *Student Sports Magazine* and Reebok. These combines began in California, have spread to Florida, and will soon be conducted in twenty-six states. The combines are usually held in late spring, and high school juniors (soon to be seniors) are invited to participate.

I've become involved in this program because in a camplike setting we've been able to create a low-pressure environment in which young athletes can receive instruction, develop some of their athletic skills, and demonstrate their talents to the college football coaches who are invited to attend the event. It's a great opportunity for students who want to be seen by as many college coaches as possible. At the same time, we give the athletes information about the recruiting process, the importance of academics, and let them know what they have to do in their senior year to make the leap to college-level sports.

For our combines, we ask high school coaches in the area to recommend their top athletes to attend the event. Best of all (from the student's point of view), it's absolutely free. It's a great opportunity for students who don't have the financial resources to attend a college-sponsored camp. Other combines are out there, but not only can they be expensive, I've found that too many of them have "meat-market"-like atmospheres. With our program, however, it's very positive, the athletes feel empowered—and the expenses are paid by the sponsors.

WAITING FOR A RESPONSE

As you and your family send out your letters (with transcripts and videos) to college coaches, also write letters to the admissions offices of these colleges, requesting general information about admissions and financial aid. Not only will you receive colorful brochures and thick catalogs in response to your correspondence, but at the same time you'll probably also begin to get letters from the coaches to whom you wrote. They might be form letters, but in many cases the coaches will write something more personal. The envelopes might include a brochure for the university's summer camp and a personal note. That could be the start of a fruitful relationship.

If you get no reply, however, do some soul searching on what that could mean. Of course, it could indicate nothing more than the coach has not had a chance to read her mail. But it may mean instead that this particular coach and college aren't really interested in meeting your needs—and thus is this a college you would want to go to anyway? One way to begin to pare down your list of twenty is to cross off the schools that haven't shown enough interest and courtesy to respond to your letter.

A FOLLOW-UP PHONE CALL

There is another option that I strongly recommend: About ten days after you expect your letter and video to arrive on the coach's desk, have one of your parents make a phone call to him or her. Fathers and mothers are usually a little apprehensive about making these calls. But they're not phoning to be meddling parents or marketing gurus. The nature of the call will make it clear that your dad or mom isn't a "pushy" parent. Here's how the conversation might begin:

"Coach Walsh, I'm Bill Johnson. I sent you a packet of information about my daughter Jenny on February tenth. I want to make sure you received the packet and I wonder if you've had time to review the contents yet."

By then, perhaps the coach has already glanced at the letter and watched the video. But in some cases, he may not have even opened the envelope yet. No matter what the situation, your dad or mom shouldn't put any pressure on the coach.

"I know you get a lot of mail, Coach, but when you do get the time to review the letter, the transcript, and the video, we'd appreciate hearing your comments. If you'd like, I could give you another call next Tuesday or Wednesday, at a time convenient to you."

CHARTING YOUR CORRESPONDENCE

During the upcoming weeks and months, you will be sending and receiving lots of mail to and from the colleges and athletic programs in which you're interested. It's important to keep the correspondence in an accessible place (perhaps a large manila envelope in your desk drawer). I also suggest being as organized as possible about this exchange of information. Keep track of all your correspondence and calls by using a chart like the following one for each college you contact.

College:
Name of Coach:
Date of Our First Letter:
Date (and Nature) of Coach's Response:
Date I Returned Player Questionnaire:
Dates of (and Reasons for) Our Subsequent Letters:
Dates of Phone Calls to College:
Dates (and Content) of Subsequent Letters from Coach:
Date of Summer Camp:

Listen to the reply, tone of voice, and overall receptivity of the coach. Sometimes, the coach's response over the phone may be much more than you had expected. "Yes, Mr. Johnson, I did get a chance to look at your packet. Actually, according to NCAA rules, we're not allowed to phone you until July first, after your daughter's junior year. But since you called us, I'm more than happy to talk to you. First of all, thank you for such a complete packet. I'm impressed with what you and your daughter sent, and there are lots of things in the video that I like. I'd love to find out more about her. And if she's interested in coming to our camp, I'd enjoy the opportunity to get to know her better. By the way, I wish all of my recruits would be so thorough. Collecting transcripts and other material can be a hassle."

You have achieved your first goal: mutual respect. And instantly you've created a balanced playing field.

From that point on, follow the coach's lead, and continue to nurture the relationship. You've opened the door and begun a dialogue. You've taken control of the process and avoided being one of those students who sits back, waits for recruiting to unfold around him, and "keeps his options open." In the next chapter, I'll discuss how to take the process to the next step.

WOMEN AND COLLEGE SPORTS

At the college level, women have always been second-class citizens when it comes to sports. As recently as the 1960s, swimmer Donna de Varona competed in two Olympics (winning a gold medal in the 400-meter individual medley), but then retired because there were no opportunities available to her competing at the college level. She was recently quoted as saying, "I came back from the Olympics and didn't have a future. All my male friends were excited about getting their way paid to Stanford and Indiana, and I had to quit as a senior in high school."

Fortunately that is changing—and changing very fast. Parity between the sexes is on its way, just as it should be. And that means many more opportunities for women, not only to compete at the college level but to earn athletic scholarships.

The impetus behind this dramatic change is a congressional mandate called Title IX, which was part of a larger piece of education legislation passed in the early 1970s and then reaffirmed in a civil rights act passed in 1988. This law bans gender discrimination in educational institutions that receive federal funding. That's why girls' sports have grown so dramatically in high schools and why they're expanding in colleges as well.

Women's college basketball has probably developed most quickly, and softball is not far behind. Swimming has been a major women's sport for several years, and many others—including soccer, crew, volleyball, water polo, ice hockey, and track and field—are expected to grow tremendously in the latter half of the 1990s, elevated from the status of club sports to full intercollegiate programs competing at the NCAA level. In colleges where women make up 50 percent of the student body, for example, they must move toward increasing participation among women to 50 percent in varsity sports, or at least meeting the level of interest in sports among women at that institution. As this happens, men's athletic programs on some campuses will suffer, and a few men's sports may be dropped completely. But college coaches in women's sports will have bigger recruiting budgets and many more scholarships to offer, all in the move toward gender equity.

CHAPTER 7

THE RECRUITING PROCESS INTENSIFIES

As the pace of the recruiting season intensifies, you'll begin to feel the excitement building. Up to this point, in the early weeks and months of recruiting, you've been doing your own research about the colleges you'd like to attend, you've sent letters, transcripts, and videos to those schools, and perhaps you've made plans to attend a camp in the summer before your senior year. You or your parents may have already called one or more college coaches after you've mailed them a packet of materials about yourself.

Before the date finally arrives when coaches are permitted to initiate phone calls to your home, they've done months and even years of canvassing athletes in your graduating class. They've collected information from high school coaches and independent scouting services, and reviewed and filed questionnaires completed by hundreds and perhaps even thousands of young athletes. They've also watched many high school games, although NCAA regulations limit the number of times they can evaluate a particular player (in most sports, it is up to four evaluations each academic year; in Division I football, the limit is two). As the recruiting season intensifies, college coaches already know most (and probably all) of the players they most want to recruit that year.

When summer arrives, coaches and incoming high school seniors can finally begin meeting and communicating with one another regularly. When I was recruiting, I really enjoyed those first contacts with my top candidates. Sure, I already knew a lot about all of them, but I believed it was important to develop a personal rapport with each player and his family.

THE FIRST CALL

When the phone rings with your initial call from a college coach, it's always a memorable experience. Imagine how astonished you'd feel to hear the voice of a bigger-than-life football coach whom you've seen on television or read about in the newspapers for years. Picture how excited you'd feel to get a call from a basketball coach who led her team to the women's NCAA Final Four the previous season. With your heart pounding, it's probably something you and your parents would never forget.

After each of those calls, your mom and dad may excitedly ask, "What'd he say? This is too good to be true! What'd he say?" However, don't allow yourselves to become too euphoric: That evening, the same coach might have two to three dozen other potential recruits on his list to call. Even so, this is probably just the first of a series of conversations that you and the coach will have over the upcoming weeks and months.

As I've already mentioned, the NCAA has guidelines on when that first phone call can take place. It cannot occur any earlier than July 1 before your senior year (or August 15 for Divisions I and II football), although *letters* from Divisions I and II schools can be sent on or after September 1 of the start of your *junior* year. Once the July 1 date arrives, coaches can call no more than once a week in all sports except football (in Division I football, the NCAA permits an unlimited number of calls from coaches during so-called contact periods).* When that first call is made, you officially become a "recruited prospective student-athlete" at that particular college, according to NCAA regulations. (Keep in mind that the recruiting dates and regulations mentioned throughout this book may change from year to year; refer to the current issue of the *NCAA Guide to the College-Bound Student Athlete*, available from the NCAA, for the latest rules.)

*In Division I football, contact periods in 1996–97 were: December 1–December 23; January 2–January 4; and January 10–February 1. There are also a few circumstances in which coaches can call you on an unlimited basis, no matter what the sport, including: (a) during the five days just before your official visit to a college campus; and (b) during the first National Letter of Intent signing date in your sport through the two days after that signing date. You (or your mother or father) can call a coach at your own expense as often as you wish, and coaches can even accept collect calls from you after the July 1 date following your junior year.

WHAT WILL YOU TALK ABOUT?

As a college coach, when I would make my first call to a particular athlete, I'd try to get acquainted with him and his family, let them know of my interest, and wish the student well in the upcoming high school season. In subsequent calls, I'd inform each student of where we were in the recruiting process—and just where he stood in our plans. I'd also "take his pulse" on what was happening in his life—and not only in sports. We'd talk about academics and how he was doing in the classroom. We'd discuss his plans for taking the SATs and the ACTs. If his sport was in season, I'd ask how he did in his games since we had last spoken. I'd inquire about other colleges he might be considering, and who else was recruiting him. Over time, I'd try to determine how close this young athlete was to making a decision about coming to my university (or another one).

During that first call, I'd always tell the student, "If your dad and mom are at home, I'd love to talk to them." I believe it is as important for the recruiter to get to know the parents as the student, and keep all of them apprised of the recruiting process that's unfolding.

Even if the college coach doesn't ask to speak to your parents, look for an opportunity where you can turn the phone over to them. In that first conversation, your father or mother could say something like:

"Coach Smith, I just want to introduce myself. I know it's early in the recruiting season, but I hope in the weeks ahead you'll help educate me a little with respect to your particular college and answer any questions I have. My daughter's worked really hard in school, we're very proud of her, and we're excited about her senior year. I know that recruiting can be a fun process, but it can get complicated, too. So I'm interested in coming to know you a little better, Coach, and I hope you'll be agreeable to having me call you if I have any questions or concerns. I certainly won't abuse that privilege, but I hope you'll be available if we need any information."

Almost immediately, you're going to find out how important you and your family are in that coach's life, and whether he's willing to spend time to answer questions that you may have.

At times, when we knew from the firing of the starting gun that a particular student was at the very top of our recruiting list, I was never shy about communicating that information. On the very first call, I might say something like, "Robert, I want you to know that we've already seen you on film, we've watched you practice, we've got your transcript. We really like what we see. Don't even worry about your senior year as it relates to our program, because we've identified you as a player we can't live without. We hope to see you here next year."

FITTING PHONE CALLS INTO YOUR LIFE

Throughout these contacts with coaches, try to keep them in perspective and don't let them become disruptive of everything else going on in your life. A weekly call from an assistant coach—and even occasionally from the head coach herself—is certainly flattering and ego boosting. But particularly if you have several colleges courting you, those phone calls can start to feel like an intrusion after a while.

By all means, feel free to "negotiate" just when these calls occur. When I was recruiting, I'd always ask the student and his family, "I'd like to phone you once a week if you're agreeable to that; a good time for me would be Sunday evenings at five o'clock if that works out for all of you." Don't hesitate to suggest a day and time that's comfortable for you and your family. Choose a time that won't interfere with homework, practices, and family obligations and activities.

ABIDING BY NCAA RULES

Here are some important points to keep in mind from the NCAA's regulations regarding recruiting:

- Boosters or alumni of a college *cannot* be involved in your recruiting. For example, boosters cannot make phone calls or send letters to you.
- You (or a family member) may not receive any benefits— including cash, clothing, cars, gifts, improper expenses, or loans—to encourage you to sign a National Letter of Intent or attend a particular college or university.

AN ONGOING ROLE FOR YOUR PARENTS

Even with the most highly recruited athletes, there's a give-and-take that occurs between student and college coach. But as I've already suggested, your parents need to become active participants, not onlookers, in this process. First of all, there's nothing more precious to parents than their son or daughter; they should be there to guide and protect you, particularly through a recruiting process that so often seems shrouded in mystery. With their life experience, adults can bring balance and maturity to the recruiting process, even though they may not understand every intricacy of recruiting. They'll hear things differently than you will, and should really oversee recruiting for the family. Appoint them as the head of your recruiting team

Let's face it: Most seventeen- and eighteen-year-olds are at a disadvantage when talking with an adult who is seeking, not giving, information. This becomes a one-sided call that tips the scales in favor of the coach. That must not happen. The scenario should be one of mutual respect and an exchange of information. A parent can help keep your family on a level playing field—eyeball to eyeball—with the coaching staff. Particularly if the coach isn't offering the information you want about how you measure up and when final decisions are going to be made, your parents should ask the tough and relevant questions such as:

- "Have you completed the evaluation process of this year's recruiting class?"
- "Where does my son/daughter rank within that class?"
- "When will you extend offers?"

It's best to know exactly where you stand, and questions like these can help you get to the bottom line. However, your parents should pace their questions so they aren't coming in a machine-gun, rapid-fire manner. They should listen carefully to the responses and take notes. Similar to my suggestion in chapter 6 about keeping a log about your written correspondence with colleges, I also advise you to do the same relative to your phone calls and conversations with coaches, noting their names, the dates and times of these calls, and what transpired.

So each time a coach calls, once you have spoken to him or her, continue making the comfortable transition to putting your father or mother on the phone. Say something like, "My dad is right here. If you don't mind, he'd like to say 'hi' and talk to you for a few moments." Most coaches, particularly if they're recruiting the right way, will always welcome the opportunity to dialogue and develop their relationship with a recruit's parents. I always felt that if this young athlete was going to spend four to five years of his life on our campus, I wanted to know as much as possible about his family; in a sense, the entire family was going to be part of our program, and I was recruiting them all.

INITIATING PHONE CONTACTS

Over the weeks, both you and your parents can also continue the dialogue with coaches by making calls of your own. However, when you make calls, be sure there's a reason for doing so. For example:

"Coach, I want to give you some updated information about me. I had two great tennis matches last week—one of them I won 6-2, 6-0, and I had seven aces. I'd love to send you the newspaper article about it."

Or:

"Coach, I thought you might want to hear that my daughter was named Cross-Country Runner of the Year by the *Times* last week. I'm going to be sending you a clipping on that, and if there's anything else I can do to help keep your file on her up to date, please let me know."

Don't become a nuisance, of course, but an occasional phone call can help solidify your relationship with a coach who has already expressed an interest in you. Also, keep in mind that, to a large degree, it's not *what* you say during these calls, but *how* you say it. If your dad is overly boastful and overbearing on the phone, for example, and his telephone demeanor sounds as though he's gotten his chest pumped up and he's engineering a full-court-press marketing campaign on your behalf, the coach on the receiving end of those calls may become annoyed by the high-pressure tactics, and it might have a negative effect on your recruitment. Yes, it's a balancing act, but if done properly, calls to the coach's office can work to your advantage.

A PERSONAL TOUCH

Phone calls aren't the only way to keep in touch with college coaches. Tim Carey, whom I worked with when he was in high school, was being recruited by Stanford and other major colleges, and at one point, the Stanford coach requested additional film of Tim in action, which we provided. A few days later, Tim received a handwritten note from Bill Walsh, who was then the Stanford head football coach. Tim sent a brief handwritten letter right back:

"I really appreciate your note, Coach. Good luck in Saturday's game."

Not many recruits do that. But it's a way to keep your name fresh in the coach's mind and to continue building rapport with the coaching staff and maintain an equal footing.

THE EVALUATION PROCESS EVOLVES

As the weeks pass, coaches will continue their evaluations of you and their other recruits—consolidating information, eliminating some names, and beginning to make decisions on others. At every college, the coaching staff—both the head and assistant coaches— has regular meetings, during which each of them updates her fellow coaches on the status of her recruits. She'll answer questions like: "How is each player doing this season? Are we still as enthusiastic about her as we were at our last meeting? Does she seem to be leaning toward our school? Who else is recruiting her? What's the relationship like with her parents?" From the college's point of view, recruiting is anything but a random process; there is real diligence on the part of the coaching staff, and careful thinking and evaluation that goes into every decision.

During your senior year, in addition to those regular phone calls, coaches may come to one or more of your games to watch you in action. And for some players, that can become unnerving. So many young athletes get anxious or concerned, figuring that this is "the big moment"—and they end up having a bad game. It shouldn't be that way. I used to call my recruits and tell them, "I'm going to be in town, and I'll be at your game Friday night. I want you to know that I'm sold on you, so don't think you have to play well for me. Go out and have the kind of game you've been playing all season long, and I'll just be there enjoying watching you."

Bear in mind that the assistant coach with whom you're probably talking isn't the final decision maker. She can (and hopefully will) go to bat for you, but everything is filtered through the head coach, who will ultimately decide to whom scholarships will be offered. You'll be ranked among the other players in your position who are being recruited. And as this evaluation process goes on, continue to ask regularly where you're ranked. If you find out you're at the top of the list, great. But even if you learn that there are three other recruits ahead of you, at least you know where you stand, and you can take that into account as you talk to coaches from other schools.

THE HOME VISIT

Coaching at Stanford allowed me access to more than 250 homes where some of America's finest young athletes resided. It was exciting for me, and I clearly sensed that the players were just as thrilled. After all, when the coach to whom you've been talking asks if he can visit you at home, you've moved a giant step closer to signing on the dotted line of a National Letter of Intent. By investing time, as well as money for a plane ticket, a rental car, and possibly a hotel room, the college is demonstrating the seriousness of its interest in you.

At times, the head coach will make the visit; but in most cases, the assistant coach who's been recruiting you will be the first to arrive on the scene, "setting the table" for a later visit by the head coach. Because you've been communicating with this coach for many weeks or months, it won't seem as though a stranger is visiting your home. You've already developed a relationship with him, and this will be a chance to finally meet one another and get acquainted face-to-face. It's also an opportunity for both of you to answer one another's questions, and to move closer to making the decision about whether you have a future at this particular school.

For some college athletic programs, a visit to your home means that you're very close to being offered a scholarship—and that offer may actually be made during the visit itself. For other colleges, the home visit is just another step in the process, and while there's definitely interest in you, the coaches may still be weeks away from finally determining whether you're the right recruit for them. Remember, you are just one person that they have their eye on, and many other athletes are being talked to.

WHAT TO ASK DURING HOME VISITS

During that home visit, make an effort to find out exactly where you stand. The coach will certainly be asking you questions, most of which you've probably heard before: "Who else is still talking to you? . . . What other schools are you thinking about? . . . When do you think you'll be making your decision? . . . What factors are you considering in reaching your decision?" At the same time, this home visit is a perfect opportunity for your family to get an update on what the coach is thinking. It feels good to hang on to a dream—people really do often hear only what they want to hear—but it's better to know exactly what that college's needs still are and find out precisely how you fit into that picture.

Make sure you get all your questions answered. Pose those questions in a comfortable (not interrogating) tone as part of the conversation and listen carefully to the responses. Here are some of the questions you should ask:

- "Have you completed your evaluation process of this year's recruiting class?"
- "Exactly where do I rank within that class?"
- "Who are your returning players at my position?"
- "Will those athletes be playing ahead of me at that position?"
- "How many athletes do you need at my position?"
- "Historically, how often do freshmen come into your program and start?"
- "Are you going to be offering me a trip to your campus?"
- "How many scholarships are available?"
- "When will you extend offers?"

The answers to these questions will immediately elevate the recruiting process. In most cases, the coach will appreciate the serious and knowledgeable way in which you're approaching your future.

THE POST-VISIT ANALYSIS

Once the coach leaves your home, sit down with your parents and conduct a mini-evaluation of what went on during the visit. Sort out what the coach said to you—and what she may have left unsaid. What did you like about the scenario she painted for you? Are there any questions that remain unanswered?

Frankly, after a coach comes into your home, if you don't know where you stand in the recruiting process once she has left, you and your parents haven't posed the right questions. Yes, it's tough to ask, "Exactly where do I stand?" But it's even harder to feel as though you're in recruiting limbo, not knowing whether you're going to be offered a trip to the campus and/or a scholarship. And if the coach doesn't seem willing to make a commitment, ask her, "I'm really interested in attending your school; what can we do now to move me closer to that goal?" Together, you may be able to devise a plan of action that can help you reach your own dreams.

ARE YOU STILL IN THE RUNNING?

In the ensuing weeks, the coach who visited will probably continue to call each week. At the same time, other coaches may visit your home, and you'll begin to pare down your own list of schools that you're still considering. Tell each coach what's happening ("I'm trimming my list, and I've just had one trip set up; I'm excited about the way things are going, but I'm still very interested in your college"). Your feedback may force the coach to move more quickly on a decision about you before she gets squeezed out of the running.

Of course, at some point in this process—perhaps after the home visit, or maybe earlier or later in some cases—coaches will eliminate athletes from their list of recruits. If you haven't heard from a coach for a three-week period, have a parent get on the phone and call her. Again, your intention is to find out what is happening and whether she's moved on to someone else. Your dad might say, "We haven't talked in three weeks, and I'm sure you're making some decisions about your recruiting. We'd just like to know where my daughter fits into your plan at this point." Or if you feel you have some leverage to stir into the recruiting pot, do it: "I don't know what your current thinking is about my daughter, but I want you to know that she has had three trips offered—by colleges X, Y, and Z—but because she's still very interested in your college, we've been reserving a trip to your campus." (By the way, make sure you've really been offered these other trips and that they've been officially scheduled; coaches talk to each other as they're tracking the recruiting process.)

Naturally, you're hoping to hear that you're still in the running and on the brink of being made an offer of a campus visit or a scholarship. Perhaps your phone call will prompt a coach to make a decision in your favor. However, even if her interest is elsewhere, a "no" at least allows you to position yourself more knowledgeably with the schools still recruiting you. Be grateful when a coach is honest enough to say, "We have two other players at your position in front of you. We haven't ruled you out yet, and we hope you're still interested. But if we do make you an offer, it won't be for at least two to three weeks."

That's a very valuable piece of information. You want to know who's still considering you and who isn't so you can make decisions that are in your own best interest. I believe that coaches have an ethical obligation to call with bad news as well as good, but they often don't. For most recruiters, the most difficult part of their job is telling a high school senior, "I'm sorry, but we have nothing for you." They do become emotionally attached to the young people they recruit, and it's hard to explain that they're no longer interested—so many of them just stop calling instead. As much as possible, however, you need to know what every coach is thinking every step of the way, even if sometimes it means finding out that you won't be getting an offer.

VISITING COLLEGE CAMPUSES

"Kylee, this is Coach Rogers. I'm calling to invite you to visit our campus next month. We're very interested in you, and would like you to see our school and our athletic facilities."

A phone call like that is precisely the kind you and your family have been working months and even years to receive. Without a doubt, this college has a strong interest in you. That's very exciting— but a trip carries no guarantees. If you ask what the invitation means, the assistant coach who's been recruiting you may say, "We're offering you this trip because we're very serious about you. But as you know, I don't have the power to make the final decision— only the head coach does—and our policy is that the coach makes the formal offers on our campus." Other schools and other coaches may make you that offer shortly before or after your trip (perhaps during the coach's visit to your home). Find out what each college's procedure is for making offers.

During your senior year, you can make up to five expense-paid college trips, no more than one to any single campus, with each visit lasting as long as forty-eight hours. (You can visit other campuses on your own at your own expense.) The college will pay for your round-trip transportation, and your meals, lodging, and tickets to campus athletic events. I suggest that one or both of your parents accompany you on these college visits (although the school can't pay for their plane tickets, it may provide their meals and lodging). If you're like most high school students, you'll probably cringe at the thought of what the coaches and other recruits might think of you because your parents tagged along. But during that weekend, you're really not going to see mom and dad very much—they'll be socializing with other parents and attending meetings arranged for them. But believe me, you'll actually *want* to see them because there's so much you'll enjoy discussing with them, and so much excitement that you'll want to share.

WHAT HAPPENS AT THE COLLEGE CAMPUS?

During your visit, depending on your sport and the particular college's policy, you might be one of five, fifteen, twenty-five, or more players brought in that same weekend. You and the other recruits will be picked up at the airport by an assistant coach or another representative of the athletic department. You'll attend a general reception with the head coach, where everyone will be introduced (including your parents). You'll be guests at a dinner that night, and then at a sports event (perhaps a basketball game) if one is being held on campus. The next morning, you'll have breakfast with your position coach, while the head coach floats from one table to the next. There will also be time for presentations from academic advisers, students from your major (if you've declared one), and a film about the university. There will probably also be an hour or two of free time a day when you can just walk around the campus on your own, peek into the library, classrooms, and the student union, talk with some students about academic life, and just get a better feel for the campus than the glossy brochures can provide.

Before the trip, ask the assistant coach making the arrangements if there's any special attire you should bring with you ("Will there be a formal function I'll be attending?"). Also, because of both legalities and liabilities, don't expect to be invited by the coach to shoot a few hoops in the gymnasium, or run the length of the football field; if an athlete seriously injured a knee, for example, during this type of activity, he and his family would probably be talking to attorneys for months or years. So bring some workout attire if you want to go jogging on your own during your free time; you won't be issued any sweats or other gear by the college itself.

You'll probably be hosted by players from the present team; you'll even get the chance to live in a dorm with them (or stay in a nearby hotel) and perhaps attend one of their parties. Along the way, you'll get a good sense of whether you fit in—and the players will probably tell you exactly what they think of the program. You might hear, "This is the greatest university; you'll really be happy if you come here." Or perhaps a disgruntled player may say, "Nobody likes the coach," which may be an outgrowth of a series of her own disappointments that have created a bias that may or may not be legitimate. Remember, the coach is putting on her best face while recruiting, but her current players may tell you what the program is *really* like there. Look, listen, and absorb as much information as possible about the school, professors, coaches, and players.

TIME TO MEET THE COACH

Sometime during the weekend, you (and your parents) will get a chance to sit down in the head coach's office and meet with him or her privately. This meeting might last fifteen to thirty minutes, depending on how many recruits the coach needs to meet and talk with. You'll get a chance to ask any questions you have, while he or she will try to evaluate your intentions. If your parents have made the trip with you, the coach may relate to you differently than if you've arrived alone; rather than simply listening to the coach give little more than a pep talk ("This is a wonderful school, we have a wonderful program, and we think you're a wonderful player!"), your parents should be better able to steer the conversation to answer questions like, "We think Kylee is a talented athlete, too, but are you in a position to offer her anything today?" Much too often, *general* information about scholarships is discussed, but not a scholarship *offer*. Parents frequently avoid the specific question, "Are you offering my son/daughter a scholarship?"

Of course, you're hoping that the coach will be honest with you. But that isn't always the case, and you should look for signs of sincerity—and insincerity. A head coach is probably being candid if she says something like, "Kylee, you've met all our coaches and seen our facility, and we'd like you to come here. But we're probably going to bring in another player at your position this year, too, and probably others every year after that. We want you to compete for that position, and we're going to give you every opportunity to win the starting job."

With some coaches, however, sincerity is elusive. They might say, "Kylee, we're not going to recruit anyone else at your position while you're here with us. You can count on that." Actually, about all you can count on is eventually learning that there are one or more other recruits at your position, participating in the first practice right alongside you—no matter what you've been told.

HOW TO DEAL WITH THE COACH'S PRESSURE

At times, you may feel you're being unfairly pressured by the coach, who might say, "I'm making you an offer today, but there are three other athletes out there we have identified, along with you, as great players. We don't think we can lose with any of you, and so the first one who says 'yes' is going to get the scholarship. So I really need your answer today, or within twenty-four hours after you get home. I hope you're ready to say 'yes,' because I can't control what the other three are going to do." In fact, that may genuinely be the situation, particularly if the coaching staff has been honest in its conversations with you up to that point. But the coach might also be trying to coerce you into making a quick decision and canceling other campus visits where you might be tempted to choose another school.

If you still want to take those other trips—and they're really firm commitments—be sincere and tell the coach that. "Coach, I really appreciate the offer, and I'm very excited by it. But to be fair to myself, I'm going to investigate the other schools that have invited me to their campuses. I hope you'll wait until then before you make a decision, but if you can't, I understand." (This type of statement might be hard for you to say, which is one reason why your parents are there; they may be better able to express exactly how you feel.)

The coach should respect your decision. Hopefully, she'll respond by saying something like, "You owe it to yourself to find out what is best for you, so take the time you need. But I'd like to stay in close contact with you and your family as we begin making decisions as well."

Here's a warning, however: Don't play poker unless you've got the hand to play with. Be sure you've really got other offers waiting for you and that you're not saying "no" to your only sure thing. Every year, I talk to athletes who have been locked out because options they thought were genuine weren't real after all.

To further complicate matters, some coaches offer an official trip on a date in the future, which leaves the college a route of "escape." For example, this trip may be scheduled toward the end of the recruiting season, but as you wait for that date to arrive—and even though it appears all is well—one of the coach's priority recruits may commit to that college in the meantime, and your trip will be canceled! Please ask if you don't know exactly where you stand in the process.

CUTTING THE PROCESS SHORT

Most students find that these college trips wear thin after a while. The first couple are fun, but then they start to become tiring. Many students begin to feel exhausted by it all and recognize that after many months of talking to recruiters they actually knew early in the game which college they want to attend. You might be ready to make your decision *before* you've taken advantage of all your invitations. So if a coach offers you a scholarship on one of those trips, seriously consider accepting it and canceling your other invitations, unless you still haven't visited the college that's your number-one choice.

As you've noticed, I don't believe in a young person visiting colleges just for the sake of traveling. Much or all of the evaluating and comparing of schools can be done in your own home, in the same way that colleges are screening you in their athletic offices. The longer the recruiting process extends, the more that can go wrong. So if you can get a commitment on the phone from a coach, and she formally extends an offer to attend her school, jump at the opportunity if that's where you really want to go to college. The sooner you can bring the process to a close, the better.

I've always thought of recruiting as a choreographed dance. When you get invited to make those campus trips, it's like going to the formal with the best-looking girl (or guy) at school—and what kid doesn't want to keep on dancing? But eventually, it has to come to an end, and you have to make a decision. There's no need to prolong the process if you really know what your decision's going to be.

By the way, if you *haven't* received an offer or made a commitment during a college visit, the coaches who are still interested in you will continue to call you. They should let you know how their own recruiting efforts are falling into place, and you should do the same.

WHAT ABOUT UNOFFICIAL VISITS?

If you're considering colleges in your general geographic area, you can make unofficial visits on your own. The NCAA places no limits on trips to college campuses made at your own expense. During the summer, for example, you and your family can schedule a vacation with stops at five or six colleges that would fit your needs as a student and an athlete. You can even call the coach in advance, let her know when you're going to be passing through, and ask if you can stop by her office and introduce yourself. (Be sure you've already sent the coach a packet of information about yourself, so your name is familiar to her.)

If the coach herself is not available to meet with you during your unofficial visit, she will probably arrange to have an assistant coach or a graduate assistant give you a tour of the athletic facilities and the campus itself. Coaches realize that they're ambassadors for their universities, and even if you're not a top recruit, they should make sure that you're treated well when you're on campus. Even if you're someone who is not at the top of their recruiting list, but they still like some of what they've seen and heard about you, these one-on-one unofficial visits are a great chance for the coach to get to know you better.

By the way, after a campus visit (whether official or unofficial), write the coach a brief letter, thanking her for the hospitality and expressing your continued interest in her school (if that's the case). Sending a letter is not only the polite thing to do, it will serve as a reminder that you are still out there and hope to continue the dialogue with her. The following box is a sample of such a letter.

SAMPLE OF A POST-VISIT LETTER

Dear Coach Williams:

Thank you so much for inviting me to visit your campus last weekend. My parents and I enjoyed meeting you and some of your assistant coaches and players. I liked living in the dorm, taking part in the activities you planned, and getting a feeling for what campus life is like.

Thank you again, and I hope we can talk soon about my continuing interest in playing at your university.

Sincerely,

John J. Athlete

MAKING THE COMMITMENT

Most sports have an initial national signing date. In football, it's usually in early February (in 1997, it is February 5). In women's volleyball, field hockey, soccer, and men's water polo, it's also early February. In basketball and most other sports, it's November. That's when you'll formalize the decision of the college you'll attend and sign the National Letter of Intent. Read the document carefully before you sign, and if you have questions, ask your college coach. As a guide, refer to the National Letter of Intent in Appendix C (pages 173–79), but keep in mind that some of the "small print" may change from one year to the next, including the initial and final signing dates.

WHAT ABOUT A SCHOLARSHIP?

Be sure you fully understand the kind of scholarship or financial aid (if any) being offered to you. Again, there will be documents to sign that spell out the details of this part of the agreement. Both Division I and II schools can offer aid that covers all your college costs (Division III schools can provide similar types of aid if you can show financial need that has nothing to do with your athletic talent). Other monetary assistance (such as government funds like Pell grants, as well as student loans) may be available, too, so ask your coach (and the college's financial-aid officials) for information about these options.

Incidentally, sometimes you might be offered only a partial scholarship. In fact, in some sports, full scholarships are rarely given. Instead, you might be awarded a quarter or a half scholarship.

A student receiving a full ride gets all her college costs paid for—typically, tuition and other student fees, room and board, and books. Those on a half ride have one-half of those expenses covered. Some students have a particular portion of their college costs paid for—for instance, their scholarship may cover only room and board, only tuition, or only books. (At the college level, funds to pay for your books can be a substantial amount of money.) Many college coaches have quite a bit of flexibility in how they apportion their scholarship funds.

Keep in mind that whether in Division I or II, athletic scholarships are generally not based on a student's need for financial aid but rather on his or her athletic abilities. The scholarship is an incentive for the student to attend that university. Yet even though need is not a primary consideration for awarding these scholarships, coaches often keep a particular student's financial situation in mind when dividing up half or quarter scholarships.

In most cases, regardless of family income, the student-athlete feels a sense of belonging, validation, and status when she's offered something from the university. It's great to be wanted, but I strongly encourage recruits and their families (along with the universities) to keep the "business side" of recruiting to themselves; too often, fabricated stories arise from families who "inflate" their student's recruiting status. I believe this is family business, however, and should remain confined to the participants.

No matter what level of financial help you're offered, keep in mind that all athletic scholarships are awarded for one year. Although there are no guaranteed four-year scholarships, they can usually be renewed each year, up to a maximum of five years within a six-year period. At most schools, unless you've violated a morals clause of your contract with the college, your scholarship will almost routinely be extended from one year to the next.

Again, if you're not being offered a full ride, let the college coach know whether you'll need some additional financial aid, such as loans or grants. Be specific, saying something like, "Coach, I'm very appreciative of the half scholarship you can provide, but are there loans or grants I can also take advantage of? What other sources of money are available? Can I work?"

The coach should be able to tell you the types of funds you can access, and he can point you toward the financial-aid office and the person there with whom you can meet. Coaches know that a college education is expensive, and the savvy ones will offer advice such as, "We can give you only a partial scholarship, but there are other opportunities for financial assistance if you need it. Here is a booklet explaining the types of help available; let me know if you have any questions, and if I can't answer them, I'll find someone who can."

Also, keep in mind that if you have achieved in the classroom in high school, an *academic* scholarship may be part of your package.

Remember, while scholarships and grants do not have to be paid back, loans must be repaid. Make sure you understand in advance the repayment schedule of any loans you receive; in most cases, you won't have to begin repaying the money until you have left college.

One other note: If you are going to be applying for financial aid, including loans or grants, do so early—many months before you arrive on campus. You want the money to be there when your freshman year begins, so make sure you meet the deadlines on the applications. A single form—the Free Application for Federal Student Aid—serves as the form you'll need to fill out and submit for many federal and state aid packages, and your high school counselor can provide you with a copy of it.

SIGNING ON THE DOTTED LINE

No matter what college you finally decide to attend, the National Letter of Intent that you'll sign shouldn't be taken lightly. It is a legal document between you and the college, confirming your decision to enroll in that institution and play your sport there. Both you and your parents, as well as the college athletic director, must sign the document in triplicate. Be sure you have read and understood all of the letter fully before signing.

The National Letter of Intent is administered by the Collegiate Commissioners Association, not the NCAA. Thus, questions about the letter should be directed to the CAA (c/o Southeastern Conference, 2201 Civic Center Blvd., Birmingham, AL 35203).

After you've signed the Letter of Intent, you'll almost certainly feel a sense of relief—although there might also be a feeling of emptiness as the whirlwind of excitement subsides and you get back into the routine of high school life. Also, be prepared to deal with jealousy from some of your peers who weren't recruited. You might even find yourself second-guessing your own choice of a college on occasion; that's human nature, so don't become preoccupied with those thoughts.

The transition to the next level will be challenging. But for the next few months, enjoy your senior year of high school, and do the best you can academically (and in every other way) up to the day of graduation.

A MESSAGE FOR PARENTS

There is a lot about the recruiting process that appeals to parents. For many of them, their own egos are boosted when their sons and daughters receive letters and phone calls from college coaches. They swell with pride, and tell their friends, "*We're* getting recruited. It looks like my kid is a D-1 [Division I] recruit!"

I believe strongly that it's important for parents to play a role in the recruiting of their youngsters—but *not* in ways that make life difficult for both their children and the coaches interested in them. Yes, parents should be vigilant, stand behind their youngsters, protect them and look out for their best interests. But too often, fathers in particular put unnecessary pressure upon their children, sometimes leaving the kids thinking to themselves, "How can I ever live up to this? I'm not *that* good!" In these cases, parent-child conflicts often arise, and the youngster often ends up announcing, "I don't want to play sports anymore!" She's so relieved to finally escape from the pressure cooker.

As a parent, work toward presenting your child in the best light possible, but in an honest way. Use this book to help you understand the process, and keep a balance in your family life, while remaining humble and realistic. I enjoy working with parents who say, "I want to give my child every opportunity; I think she's good, but I know that others may be better judges than me. I just want to make sure every resource is available so she's evaluated fairly and has a great college experience." But I shy away from parents who are pushy and arrogant—and who ultimately turn off their own children. I've seen some parents tell coaches, "If you can't guarantee that my son will have the chance to lead the nation in passes thrown, we're not coming to your university." Their children are left feeling embarrassed and humiliated—and without a college to attend.

Through it all, you need to listen to your youngster, and watch her behavior. Remember, athletics is only one part of life. If she really wants to play sports in college, she'll demonstrate it in her commitment to athletics and to her schoolwork. Her actions will tell you most of what you need to know.

CHAPTER 8

WHEN YOUR PHONE ISN'T RINGING

If you are a blue-chip high school athlete, recruiting may be taking care of itself. As colleges have learned of your athletic talent, your home will become transformed into a virtual who's who of college coaches. As hectic as the process may become, you've found yourself in the enviable position of having several (and perhaps many) schools and scholarships from which to choose. Congratulations!

But what if you're not one of these super recruits? Remember, the highly sought-after players comprise only a minority of the six million students playing high school sports. Many more young athletes are not stars on their high school teams—nor have they been written about regularly in the local papers—even though they've performed very well. Consequently, as the recruiting process unfolds each year, many thousands of talented high school players feel they're being bypassed, getting little or no attention from college coaches. As a result, they're left feeling frustrated, disappointed, and hurt.

When newspaper articles describe the colleges where the most highly recruited players are headed, it's easy for the others to feel left out and unfairly overlooked. If you're in that position, you might find yourself thinking, "No one wants me!" . . . "My high school coach didn't promote me." . . . "I'm better than that guy."

In fact, while some high school athletes do get bypassed, very few are actually *overlooked*. There's a lot of talent out there, and all high schools, including your own, have been carefully canvassed (I've described that process earlier in the book). When college coaches make their decisions and offer their scholarships, they're choosing the athletes they think meet the needs of their program. Sometimes they make the right judgments, sometimes they don't. But if you're starting to feel left out, you don't have to sit back, waiting passively for the phone to ring and clinging to the hope that fate will ultimately turn a college coach's attention toward you.

TAKING BACK CONTROL

If you feel as though you're still standing on the dock after most of the recruiting ships have pulled out, now is the time to take back control of your own future. So often I talk to high school seniors and their parents who are baffled that college coaches seem to have neglected them. At the start of their senior year, these students may have had visions of Notre Dame or Penn State dancing in their heads. They probably filled out questionnaires sent to them by college athletic departments and became convinced that they were being actively recruited. They believed they'd be in the enviable position of having to choose from among multiple scholarship offers. But after the national signing date came and went, they've felt confused, their egos have been crushed, and they're wondering why they have nothing to show but a file folder full of form letters. When they're asked, "Were you really being recruited by Notre Dame?," they typically respond, "Well, I wrote them a letter, and got one back." Unfamiliar with how recruiting works, they often complain, "I can't believe no one wants me anymore. . . . It's just not fair!"

If you were truly overlooked, however, you'd have nowhere to go. But that's not the case with *anyone* who really wants a college education. Even if your dream schools did stop calling (or never called at all), you still have choices. No matter where you stand at the moment in the recruiting process, you can't be overlooked if you're realistic about your prospects and have your academic life in order.

FACING YOUR FUTURE REALISTICALLY

As you may have already witnessed, in the sea of recruiting the big fish do their roaming with the largest boats and the most spacious nets, coming home with the most sought-after catches while tossing back what they don't want. But as you'll learn in this chapter, if you're one of those who finds yourself treading water after the top recruits have found a home, it may be time to reset your sights:

Perhaps you won't get the college scholarship you had wanted. . . . Maybe you'll end up as a walk-on rather than a highly recruited and courted prospect. . . . Perhaps you'll find that a Division II or III school fits your needs, even though you had once dreamed of attending a Division I college. Some adjustments may be necessary, but you *do* still have choices.

"Recruiting is a very difficult process for coaches," says David Tipton of Stanford. "It's not an exact science, and some good athletes do get bypassed." Even in David's own case, no one recruited him when he was in high school. So he went to a junior college instead, where he proved himself and made the leap to Stanford and then to the National Football League, where he played for six years.

So take the opportunities where you find them—even if it means going to a smaller or less prestigious college than you had once dreamed about. Sometimes, when a young athlete and his parents have envisioned only the glamour and prestige of Division I powerhouse programs, they focus on their disappointments and lose sight of the opportunities still at hand. While fathers may have viewed their 5'10", 195-pound son playing inside linebacker and becoming the next Nick Buoniconti, many college coaches wouldn't even give Buoniconti himself a second glance today because of the size requirements into which they've boxed themselves.

But don't think that obstacles like size are insurmountable—because they aren't. At a recent college football convention in Anaheim, several of my coaching friends and I were discussing what they were looking for when recruiting, and our conversation shifted to athletes (like Buoniconti) who had terrific careers but would be overlooked today by many college coaches. One of them was actually sitting there with us—Rich Glover, an undersized nose guard who redefined his position and whose coaches at the University of Nebraska were willing to let him utilize his talents fully and just let him play. And play he did, setting new standards of performance and winning the Outland Trophy.

At that meeting in Anaheim, I saw the jaws of several coaches drop when they met Glover for the first time, and were unable to contain their surprise at his size. I believe that as long as there are coaches who will go out on a limb for great players—and there still are some—room will always exist for the Rich Glovers of the athletic world. If you want to play college sports badly enough, and have the will and the heart to go along with your physical gifts, there is a place for you.

CONSIDERING YOUR ALTERNATIVES

Back in chapter 6, when you made your list of the top twenty colleges you'd like to attend, I suggested that you include some smaller schools to round out your list. That meant listing not only Division I-A colleges, but also Division I-AA, II, and III.

Back then, you may have cringed at the thought of having to settle for one of these smaller or less prestigious colleges. Some high school students assume that the numerical assignments alone—Divisions I, II, III—are reflections of the level of play at these institutions. "If you're at a Division II school, the caliber of athletic competition just isn't as good," they may think. But the fact is that while the play might be different, the lower divisions develop many quality athletes and end up sending a lot of them to the pros. Just as important (or even more so), many Division II and III schools have outstanding academic reputations and are wonderful institutions from which to earn your college degree. Remember, as much as you enjoy sports, the *real* reason for attending college is to get an education and come away with a degree that will serve you well throughout your life.

TAKING ADVICE TO HEART

If you're lucky, in the early stages of recruiting, you might have received some realistic advice and direction from one of the college coaches with whom you made contact. You and your parents may have sent a letter and videotape and followed up with a phone call, during which an honest coach may have said "no," but done so in a very helpful way. For example:

"Mr. Taylor, I appreciate the material you've sent, but I just don't think your son is going to fit into our program. We're recruiting some other kids who are further along in their athletic development than your son."

"I appreciate your candor, Coach. But let me ask you this: Where do you see my son fitting in?"

"Well, have you looked at the California State University campus up the highway? If I can make a suggestion, give a call to Steve Smith, the assistant volleyball coach there. He recruits in this area, and they do a great job with kids like yours. Tell Steve that I saw your video and thought it would be a good idea for the two of you to connect."

That kind of feedback should be music to your ears.

RECRUITING AT THE SMALLER COLLEGES

Coaches at the second-tier schools recruit just as actively as at the larger universities—distributing three-by-five cards, attending high school games, contacting students and parents, offering campus visits. But their recruiting budgets are smaller, and they often must play a waiting game. Some of the players they're interested in have had their sights set on the bigger, better-known universities—those schools that play on national television each Saturday. But once the major colleges offer their campus trips, and many talented young athletes are left without a single invitation, the recruiting game moves to the next level. As disappointed students lick their wounds, they may be contacted by these second-tier coaches who still have slots to fill. If you're one of these frustrated high school athletes, imagine how excited you'd be to hear, "We think you're an outstanding player, and we'd love you to come to our college."

When I coached at Stanford, if I saw an athlete I liked but who was lacking in the cosmetic or other departments, I spread the word to my colleagues at other universities whose programs could benefit from such a player. Interestingly, my own brother, Tim, coached at the University of Santa Clara when I was at Stanford, and he was often on the trail of these kinds of athletes even before I could tell him about my "find"! (Tim, by the way, is currently the head football coach at Portland State University.)

Many of the student-athletes I've worked with have found a home at colleges that were not originally on their top-twenty list. In fact, in some cases, they had never even heard of the colleges they eventually attended. But they turned out to be very happy with their ultimate placement—getting a lot of playing time and a good education—and in some cases, their small-college athletic experience served as a springboard to the pros. Their passion to play overcame any negatives with which some college recruiters had labeled them.

Take a look at the roster of any professional sports team, and read the names of the colleges where these top athletes competed. Jerry Rice, for example, one of the greatest pass receivers in NFL history, attended Mississippi Valley State, hardly a college renowned as a sports powerhouse. Scottie Pippen, the Chicago Bulls star, went to the University of Central Arkansas. John Stockton, the NBA's all-time assist leader, played basketball at Gonzaga College in Spokane, Washington.

When I played pro football for the Seattle Seahawks, many of my teammates had not attended the Nebraskas, Michigans, Florida States, or Notre Dames. Jim Jodat, for example, went to Carthage College. Dave Krieg attended Milton College. Others had gone to Colgate, William and Mary, Villanova, and Bowling Green. I played at the University of California at Riverside, College of San Mateo, and San Jose State (via a junior college). So the demographics of the typical NFL roster are not composed exclusively of Division I athletes. You don't have to attend a high-profile school to get noticed.

EXCELLING AT THE SECOND-TIER SCHOOLS

Some of the athletes I've worked with have had very positive experiences at smaller colleges. Gerald Wilhite (whom I wrote about in chapter 4) weighed only 98 pounds as a high school freshman, and 115 pounds as a senior. He was a talented gymnast and wrestler, but yearned to play football. When the larger universities didn't come calling, however, he ultimately found a home at San Jose State. It turned out to be a wonderful placement for both him and the university. He matured into an excellent football player, became the Denver Broncos' first-round draft selection, and played in the NFL for eight seasons.

Geoff Buffum, a quarterback at San Clemente High School, started every game as a senior and led his team to the playoffs—the first time the school had played in the postseason in thirteen years. After graduation, Geoff headed to Willamette University in Salem, Oregon, where his first collegiate pass completion resulted in an eighty-two-yard touchdown!

Another football player with whom I worked ended up as a middle linebacker at the University of San Diego (USD). For months, though, he and his parents continued to hold on to the dream that he would be offered a scholarship by a college like the University of Oklahoma or Ohio State University, even though his size (6'0", 190 pounds) worked against him. His ego was wounded, and the first time that the coach at USD called him, he wasn't particularly interested. But I reminded him, "You should be the happiest guy in America; do you know how many players don't get any calls or invitations for campus visits? You'd be tremendous at that college. I've got four players on the team, and they all love it." Immediately, his attitude changed. He visited the USD campus, was impressed with the football program, and enrolled the following school year.

Aaron Guttridge was County Football Player of the Year in 1990. At 5'10" and 220 pounds, he was an outstanding linebacker, and accepted an athletic scholarship to Idaho State University. However, because of a family tragedy, he returned home and attended a junior college. He played football at an all-American level at the JC, but nevertheless, almost no four-year colleges showed any interest in him as a transfer athlete. Aaron finally chose to attend a Division III school, Chapman College in Orange, California, which had just decided to launch a football program. He played on that inaugural squad, became team captain, the leading tackler, an all-league selection, and most important, he graduated with a college degree.

And then there's Brian Pearsall, who experienced firsthand just how unpredictable recruiting can be—but who took control of the process. Brian (whose brother, Grant, was mentioned in chapter 1) had gone through recruiting and had even made a decision to accept an offer from a particular university. The assistant coach from that college had arranged a final home visit during which he would leave the Letter of Intent and the scholarship contract with the family (the NCAA allowed this at one time). But when that day of supposed celebration arrived, no one from the university ever showed up or even phoned the Pearsall home. The coaching staff was fired, and as the coaches packed their bags, the single most important part of the process—the players—had been forgotten.

Brian had felt the sting of recruiting, although he rebounded in a mature fashion. He accepted an offer from another college—Cal Poly San Luis Obispo—and became a four-year starter there! His family also benefited in the long run, since they took nothing for granted during the recruitment of their next son.

WHAT ABOUT BECOMING A WALK-ON?

If you haven't been offered a scholarship, and you're not fighting off college coaches eager to get you on their team rosters, don't rule out the option of becoming a walk-on. Thousands of athletes in all sports become walk-ons at both large and small universities. In fact, because the NCAA now places a cap on the number of scholarships in football and other sports, more colleges are accepting walk-ons with open arms. Walking on has actually become one of the best avenues for athletes to leverage their way into a college or university.

There are two kinds of walk-ons:

- A recruited walk-on is one who has been officially recruited by the university and decides to attend that school without a scholarship. The coach clearly wants him involved in the athletic program of the university—but without any financial aid. He'll practice with the team, and if he impresses the coaches and earns a spot on the squad, he may be offered a scholarship in his second or subsequent years at the university. However, as I'll discuss in a moment, there are some concerns associated with being a recruited walk-on, and it's important to understand them early in the game.

- A true walk-on has not been officially recruited. She has been admitted to the university on her academic record alone and is then invited to early tryouts (beginning in August for fall sports) to see if she can make the grade athletically; if she does, she may be invited onto the team. It's an uphill fight, since the scholarship players are given every chance to prove they can play before walk-ons get their turn.

But with limitations on the number of scholarship players, all schools need true walk-ons to round out their teams.

THE PERILS OF WALKING ON

What's the concern surrounding *recruited* walk-ons? Some of the young athletes in this category do rise from the practice field and the sidelines to the ranks of a roster player. But most never get that far. They may take a beating in practices day after day, feeling much like a tackling dummy (as I described in chapter 4). But according to NCAA guidelines, if they ever set foot onto the field as a player in a game situation, they immediately become classified as someone who counts in the university's athletic scholarship allotment—perhaps providing them with welcome financial aid, but prompting coaches to move very carefully before elevating them to the next level and filling one of the prized scholarship slots allotted for that institution.

At many colleges, recruited walk-ons complain about feeling like "political prisoners"; coaches know that if they put these players into a game, they'll immediately count in the scholarship numbers. As a result, they often sit on the sidelines, one year after another.

Before agreeing to become a walk-on, make sure your status is declared—recruited walk-on or true walk-on. (You don't want any surprises down the road regarding your eligibility.) I advise talking with the head coach before you accept the status of recruited walk-on. Say something like, "Coach, let's talk. If I go out there during practices and prove myself—if I show that I'm better than some of the players on scholarship—will you seriously consider moving me onto the team roster and award me a scholarship?" Find out exactly where you stand—and what your prospects for the future are—*before* you enroll in school.

Also, make an effort to learn just how walk-ons are treated at the college you're considering. At some schools, they're embraced like any other athlete in the program; at others, they're ostracized and are never invited to team functions. I find this latter situation sickening and dehumanizing, but it's a reality that you should address. Discover as much as possible about the status of walk-ons, much of which will come from players already in the program. When you visit a campus, talk to the athletes there; if you find disgruntled players among the walk-ons, there's cause for concern. Ask the coach, too, how walk-ons are treated. He might refer you to players, saying something like, "I've got a guy I want you to meet; he's been in our program for three years, so rather than hearing it from me, I'd like you to talk to him." Gathering information firsthand from other students is the best way to get it.

WILL YOU EVER PLAY?

Keep in mind that as a walk-on you're facing strong odds against ever playing in a game situation. It isn't an easy road (although you'll probably earn the respect of your teammates and coaches). Even so, *every* school has a recruited walk-on or two who *does* end up making the team and contributing in a big way. Not long ago at Stanford University, Jack Gilmette became a football walk-on and not only ended up earning a scholarship but became team captain and was a starter for two seasons. Rick Neuheisel, now the head football coach at the University of Colorado, was a walk-on at UCLA during his playing days, where he worked his way into the starting quarterback position. Some coaches actually make a special effort to recognize hardworking walk-ons with scholarship dollars.

"Some students do walk on because they like both the academic and athletic programs here," says Terri McKeever. "And they may have the hope of earning a scholarship down the road."

McKeever says that every year, she makes a point of offering at least a partial scholarship to a walk-on who has proven herself. "I talk a lot to my team about the importance of personal qualities, aside from what goes on in the swimming pool, including getting good grades, having a good attitude and work ethic, being the best they can be, showing support for teammates, and helping to create an environment that enables everyone to be successful," she says. "I recently gave one of our walk-ons a partial scholarship because she does some things that I'm telling everyone are very important—and so I feel I need to reward that."

Not every coach has McKeever's attitude, however. So if you enter college as a walk-on, find out beforehand whether you have a realistic chance of earning a scholarship. Terri says, "I think that if my athletes are happy and know I care about them as people, I'll get maximum athletic performance from them. I believe you're a person first, and the athletic side of your life is just part of who you are."

HOW WALKING ON CAN OPEN DOORS

If you're undecided about joining the ranks of recruited walkons, consider this: Yes, these young athletes aren't awarded a scholarship (at least initially) and thus they're paying their own tuition, dorm costs, and other fees. But if your grades aren't quite as good as they need to be for admission to the university through normal channels, the coach may be able to open doors for you in the college's administrative offices and perhaps get you into the school as a walk-on where you would not have been admitted based on grades alone.

Let's say, for example, that you have a 3.0 GPA and scored 980 on the SATs. At some colleges, if your application was received through the normal admissions channels, you probably would not have been admitted on those academic credentials alone. But if you've proven yourself as a talented high school athlete, you may be evaluated in a different manner and win acceptance to the university.

That's one of the real benefits of being a walk-on. After all, probably thousands of students with GPAs equal to or even better than yours get rejected for admission each year. But since colleges make allowances for athletes, why not take advantage of it? Imagine getting into the school of your choice because of a combination of good (although perhaps not excellent) grades *and* athletic ability. If that happens to you, consider it a great opportunity and one of the payoffs for working hard on the high school practice and playing fields. If your parents have the financial resources to pay for your education without a scholarship—or if you get a student loan to help you out—gaining admission and getting that education have already turned you into a winner, no matter how much or how little playing time you eventually get.

Don't read the wrong message into this situation, however. There's not a college coach around who doesn't value high academic achievement in his players. He knows that intelligence is crucial in sports as well as in the classroom. There's a saying, "There's nothing more frightening than an athlete who uses his mind." A football player, for example, has to absorb and process enormous amounts of information about not only playing his own position but also about the responsibilities of each of his teammates on every play. Frankly, learning the football playbook before a game can be as demanding as studying for a test in many college academic classes.

EXPLORING THE TEAM MANAGER OPTION

There is another area of college sports worth exploring. Every athletic department has team managers, student-trainers or athletic aides who do not perform on the football field or basketball court, nor do they get their names in the box scores. But they are crucial for the functioning and the success of the program. For their contributions, they often get a full or partial athletic scholarship.

These managers or aides set up the field before practices and assist the equipment manager in a variety of activities, including laundry and packing for road games. They may be in charge of equipment for games and serve as liaisons between the athletic department and other parts of the campus. They might assist the team trainer in physical therapy programs and videotape games and practices from the sidelines or press box. They travel on road trips, stay in hotels, and are usually embraced by the athletes themselves as part of the team.

Sometimes, I'll hear high school students say, "Yes, I think I can get admitted to that university, and I could walk on. But I realize my chances of playing are small, and I'm not excited about getting battered and bruised in practices." That's when I might suggest that they consider applying for the position of an athletic aide. Depending on the particular university's standing as a Division I, II, or III school—as well as the way it has appropriated financial aid for its student trainers—they might be offered a full or partial scholarship or perhaps opportunities in a work-study program that will help pay for tuition, books, and room and board. Yes, it's a job that requires a lot of hard work, but it's a particularly worthwhile opportunity for college students interested in careers in sports administration, business management, or physical therapy. It's a job that can turn into a valuable training ground, and it'll look good on your résumé when you go hunting for your first job out of school.

When I coached at Stanford, I relied on these team managers for more than just fulfilling their assigned duties of helping to prepare for practices and games. They often had inside knowledge of what our players were thinking and feeling. In some ways, they had a much better take on team dynamics than the coaches themselves, and they were trusted members of the program who could give us insights into team morale and attitudes. Everyone recognized that these behind-the-scenes men and women were a vital part of our athletic program.

If this is a role that interests you, write a letter to the college coach in the sport that you've played in high school. Or address the letter to the athletic director. The letter should be written early—in your junior year in high school or in the fall of your senior year. Let the coach know about your own athletic background, mention that you've already applied and/or been accepted to the university (if that's the case), inquire about the program for team managers, and express your interest in being part of it. You can use the following sample letter as a guide.

SAMPLE LETTER FOR BECOMING A TEAM MANAGER

Dear Coach Jones:

I am a junior at Lincoln High School in Los Angeles. I have played varsity football for two years and also one year of JV baseball. Sports have always been an important part of my life, and I would like to continue my involvement at the college level as a team manager or aide.

I plan to apply to your university early in my senior year. My GPA in high school is 3.3, and my PSAT score was 1040. I am a member of the Boys League in high school, and in my junior year I was voted Most Inspirational Player by my football teammates. I am a hard worker and believe I can make a contribution to your athletic program as a team manager.

I have enclosed an unofficial copy of my high school transcript. I would like to find out more about how team managers are selected and utilized in your athletic department, and hope that I can become part of your program in this capacity. I will call you later this month to discuss the possibility of serving as a Trojan team manager beginning in my freshman year.

Sincerely yours,

Tom Thompson

"DO I REALLY NEED SPORTS?"

Let's consider one other alternative. Some high school athletes evaluate their situation and get a strong sense that doors they thought would be open are actually shut. Their phone isn't ringing, they aren't being invited to visit campuses, and they really aren't interested in being a team manager or aide. At that point, they step back and may decide that it's time to put sports on the shelf as they head to college.

Imagine yourself in a situation like this: Your grades are so good that you can get into UCLA on academics alone—but you probably aren't talented enough to play basketball there. At the same time, however, you could probably play at a Division II or III school, but UCLA is the college you've always dreamed of attending. In a situation like this, ask yourself, "Where do I want to graduate from?" If the answer is UCLA, then congratulate yourself on earning your way into that university and cherish the good memories of playing athletics in high school and taking advantage of sports in a positive way.

At some point in every athlete's life, your sport will "quit" you—although I'd prefer that we eliminate the word "quit" and simply consider it time to exit from competition. By choosing to exit, you will enter a new arena where you can contribute to your college and to society at large in a manner far more significant than sports. Remember, participating in athletics has taught you some valuable lessons about the value of hard work, discipline, and teamwork—qualities that will benefit you throughout life. Enjoy the feelings of achievement for all you've accomplished in sports, head off for college, and make the most of the next four years, without regret.

CHAPTER 9

WHAT TO EXPECT IN COLLEGE

When the day finally arrives that you enroll and set foot on your college campus—achieving a goal you've aimed toward for probably years—congratulate yourself on your achievement. Through hard work in the classroom and on the athletic field, you've earned entry into a college and have the opportunity for a good education and the chance to participate in a sport you enjoy.

THE NEW WORLD OF COLLEGE LIFE

In the next four to five years, you'll have some of the most exciting and memorable experiences of your life. At the same time, however, as an incoming freshman, you'll need to make some adjustments in the transition from high school to college. Yes, you've entered school with the encouragement and blessing of the college coaching staff, and perhaps you have an athletic scholarship under your arm. But relative to your sport, you need to get a realistic sense of where you fit in and how much you can begin contributing to the team, particularly in your first year on campus. During the past three to four years, you probably became comfortable with the speed and tempo of the high school game, but now you'll need to adapt to a new level of play at college, which will be more intense and competitive than what you've been used to.

You'll also be abandoning familiar surroundings—your old school and coaches, the routine of high school practices and games, longtime friends, and living at home with your family. As you leave that comfortable environment, adjustments are inevitable.

Even so, some freshmen make those adaptations with barely the blink of an eye. They enter college with an "I can do it" attitude, and they handle their new athletic and academic challenges in stride. Yet for others, the new reality hits them hard—sometimes literally. The first time a freshman running back gets pounded by a 320-pound lineman in practice, or a basketball forward has his jump shot violently swatted away by a seven-foot center, he instantly recognizes that college sports are a whole different ball game. It's a big shock for a lot of freshmen, and many of them have to deal with and overcome self-doubts that surface.

THE COACH'S VANTAGE POINT

As your own freshman year unfolds, your college coach will be watching to see how you make the transition. Some student-athletes arrive with a brash attitude and get beaten down quickly; others show up with a more cautious, tentative outlook and end up doing beautifully. You might be one of those who make a quick adjustment and whose immense talent allow them to compete immediately at the collegiate level, both athletically and academically. But some of your peers and teammates may back off, finding the transition more difficult and stressful than they expected. You never really know which category you're going to fall into until you arrive on campus. But look around, and you may see a great exodus occur as the reality and brutality of college athletics collide with the high school phenoms not equipped to handle this "new sport" (not to mention college-level academics).

When I was a college coach, I couldn't wait to finally begin working with my recruits on the football field. Yes, when they were high school seniors, I had spent time with them, believed I knew them pretty well, and had done my homework evaluating them academically and athletically, as well as judging their character. Even so, every recruiting class has surprises, and not all of them are pleasant. Yes, there is almost always an athlete or two who was lightly recruited, yet who turns into one of the most prized members of the freshman class. At the same time, there are also players who don't live up to expectations. Coaches never really know how good their recruiting class is until they watch these young athletes perform on the practice field and in game situations.

From the first day onward, coaches begin to get a sense of who belongs and who is going to struggle. In football, in a recruiting class of fifteen student-athletes, perhaps three to five ultimately end up becoming starters in a given season; a few may begin contributing as early as their freshman year, but they'll certainly play an important role in the program over the course of their four to five years at the college. Those kinds of numbers—five out of fifteen—constitute a good recruiting class. Anything better than that often means contending for a conference title and a bowl bid!

A LITTLE ADVANCE PREPARATION

As I've emphasized, be prepared to make some adjustments as you move on to college life. Remember, on the athletic field, you'll be dealing with a new level of coaching. In high school, your coach might have been a classroom teacher most of the day and put on his coach's hat only in the afternoon when practice started. Or she might have been a walk-on coach, earning her living at another job away from campus. But at college, you'll be guided by professional coaches—that is, men and women whose full-time jobs are coaching the football, basketball, softball, or field hockey team. This is their life and their livelihood, and they probably approach it with a very serious attitude.

Before you arrive on campus, you should have established at least some level of relationship with your college coach. He or she can help make your transition as smooth as possible by providing you in advance with information about the team you're joining. In fact, once you've signed your National Letter of Intent, ask for an off-season conditioning program that fits in with the coach's philosophy. Become acquainted with the terminology (in terms of play calling, for example) so you'll have a head start on your fellow recruits. Request play books that you can study over the summer and even videos that you can watch. Your goal should be to indoctrinate yourself into the style of play of the program where you'll spend the next four to five years. Competing at the college level is like entering gladiator school; it's tough and a lot more intense than high school. No one is going to hold your hand, and so if you can arrive prepared both physically and mentally, you'll feel more confident as you join the program.

THE PACE OF THE NEW ROUTINE

Once you're on campus and practices begin, your life as an athlete will move at a faster pace. Your older teammates—the sophomores, juniors, and seniors—obviously have advantages over you. Whether or not they're starters, they're familiar with the system and the coaches' tone and style. And, of course, they also have more experience practicing and playing at the college level. No matter how impressive your own talent and how highly recruited you were, you're going to feel like a novice as you gradually assimilate into the sports program.

You'll also be confronted with more structure than you may have anticipated. If you're participating in a fall sport, you'll probably be asked to arrive on campus in August to begin intense twice-a-day practices. You can also expect early wake-up calls according to the coach's schedule, not yours. Once school starts, for example, even if your first class is at 10:00 A.M., you may have a team check-in and breakfast in the dining hall at 7:00 A.M. As a freshman, you'll have to earn the privilege of more autonomy, but before that happens, you'll live by *their* rules.

Mentally prepare yourself now for a schedule that might go something like this: Mandatory wake up at 6:30, and check-in at 7:00 for breakfast. Attend classes, which might last until noon or 1:00 P.M. Grab lunch and then head for the locker room. Get taped and arrive at a team or position meeting by 2:00. Show up on the field by 2:30, and practice until 5:30 or 6:00. Then spend an hour in the weight room before going to the dining hall for dinner. After you eat, there's a mandatory study hall until 10:30. Finally, it's time for some well-needed rest—and anticipating the same cycle of events beginning the following morning. You'll also have to adjust to road trips, taking books with you when you travel, and studying on the plane or bus and in the hotel room.

Yes, it's a rat race, particularly during your sport's season. I strongly recommend that somehow, in this hectic schedule, you take care of yourself—eat properly and get as much rest as possible. At night, when your new college buddies are encouraging you to party late into the night, turn out the lights and get your rest instead. Sleep is the time when crucial body chemicals such as the human growth hormone are secreted; seven hours of sleep is good, but eight hours is better—and whenever you can squeeze in nine or ten hours, better still.

WHERE DO YOU STAND?

Before you show up for your first practice as a freshman, you should have a sense of where you fit into the coach's plans. During your campus visit in your senior year of high school, and in phone conversations with the assistant coach recruiting you, he should have told you how the program plans to use your talents. If you were an outstanding football pass receiver in high school, you probably were recruited by a college where you'd eventually get the chance to catch eighty passes a season (although probably not in your freshman year). As a basketball recruit, you learned the type of offense the coach runs, and were drawn to one that takes advantage of your own strengths. There shouldn't be any surprises in that regard during your college career.

At the same time, you should have an understanding of who might be playing ahead of you in your first year or two on campus. As I've suggested, you should have learned during recruiting who the returning players will be at your position, who has the inside track for the starting job, and traditionally how often freshmen have come into the program and started.

Coaching staffs view each athlete as being on a four- or five-year track. You'll evolve as an athlete during that time, and thus in your freshman year you might do more sitting than playing (most freshmen do, depending on the needs of the program). In strong football programs, for example, it is rare for an offensive lineman or a quarterback to be elevated to a starting position as a freshman. Even so, unexpected injuries do occur, and if the athlete or two playing ahead of you go down, you'll find yourself put into a game situation in an instant. Be prepared so you can respond if you're thrown into a fire.

Of course, there are a few college freshmen who are destined to be immediate starters. Cade McNown entered UCLA from Lake Oswego, Oregon, and after meeting with him for less than thirty seconds I was convinced he would start as a freshman—which, in fact, he did. Sports have always allowed athletes to demonstrate talent that cannot always be measured in a tangible sense.

WHAT TO EXPECT

As I've already written, no matter where you find yourself in the team hierarchy, those first few weeks may be both physically and emotionally draining, competing on the same practice field with twenty-one- and twenty-two-year-old athletes. In high school, playing your game probably felt as comfortable as pedaling a bicycle with training wheels—only to have them suddenly removed as you move to the college level; for a while, you're going to feel some unsteadiness and insecurity on the bike until you become at ease with your new situation. Yes, the basics—two wheels, pedals, and handlebars—are the same, but getting the feel for the next level takes time, and you can only do that by falling off and getting back on. Some of that will inevitably occur as you embark on your college playing career.

Fortunately, in most college athletic programs, coaches have created a mentor program in which a junior or senior will take you under her wing and play a leadership and support role in your own adjustment. Rather than razing or hazing, the good programs reach out to their freshmen to make them feel welcome and part of the team. During the recruiting process itself you should have learned from the college coach just what to expect in that regard.

Nevertheless, even if you've asked your coach to look at playbooks during the summer before your freshman season, you're still not going to be up to speed with the athletes who have already been there for two, three, and four years. To compound this disadvantage you're experiencing, freshmen in the football program miss spring practice, which is held while they're still high school seniors; that's twenty days of preparation they've lost, which leaves them playing catch-up once school starts in the fall. In a sense, the deck is stacked against you—but I've found that most coaches will still give you every opportunity to prove yourself, beginning on the first day you put on the practice uniform. They were probably being very honest if during recruiting they told you, "We're going to give you a fair chance to come in and earn playing time and even a starting position as a freshman. But if you're not ready for the transition, we believe strongly in preserving another year for most of our freshmen."

WHAT ABOUT REDSHIRTING?

"Son, we've evaluated our talent this season and we don't believe you fit into our immediate plans. We've decided to redshirt you this year."

For some student-athletes, their first reaction to that kind of news is emotional devastation. After all, they may have had dreams of excelling as freshmen and playing on Saturday afternoons. And suddenly that bubble is burst.

But while you may indeed feel some initial disappointment, redshirting can be a wonderful opportunity. Think of it: You'll save a year of eligibility for a later time when you're more polished and poised as an athlete, and if you're on scholarship, you'll get a fifth year of education free. That could mean extra time to insure that you get your bachelor's degree, or if you're on track academically, it's an opportunity to use your additional year at school for postgraduate studies.

WHAT YOU CAN GET OUT OF REDSHIRTING

Frankly, most young athletes benefit from a year of redshirting. In a sense, I think of redshirting as a prize or reward. It's a sign that the coaching staff has decided to invest in you and your future in their program, and they have the patience to let you develop. Yes, they may see some immaturity, physically and emotionally, as you entered as a freshman. But they've concluded that with an extra year to evolve and mature, they can nurture you along to a point where you can make your greatest contribution to their program. That's quite a different situation from the freshman who comes in and impresses no one and is going to be pushed through the program as quickly as possible; rather than giving him or her an extra year to develop as a redshirt, the coaches are going to get him or her out in four years, while grumbling over having made a recruiting mistake.

So some freshmen athletes size up the team, talk to the coach, and conclude, "I'm going to give it my best, but I'll probably benefit most by redshirting for a year." As a redshirt, you'll continue to practice with the team, and depending on the college and sport, you may suit up with your teammates for home games and cheer them on from the sidelines (for road games, you'll probably stay home because of limitations on the number of players who can travel).

What's my advice if you're asked to redshirt your freshman year? Jump at the opportunity. It's important, however, not to slide through that year. Yes, in the coach's mind, you may be third, fourth, or fifth in the depth chart at your position. But if you practice very hard and impress the coach with your work ethic, you'll move up the ladder. Inevitably, there will be moments of frustration as a redshirt. On game days, this may be the first time in your sports career that you've sat on the bench; throughout high school, you were probably always a starter, and now you're watching from the sidelines. But hopefully your coach will be sensitive to what you're experiencing. I remember telling my redshirt athletes, "You're going to be a great player for us. We believe in you. Hang in there; your hard work will pay off."

So keep your eye on the prize. Follow the training program prescribed by your coach, and refer back to chapter 2 for some additional training guidelines that can enhance your vision, balance, power, flexibility, and speed. Outwork your competition, even if you aren't listed in the game program. In the next one, two, or three years, your time will come. Just ask Gil Byrd (whom I wrote about in chapter 4)!

WHAT ABOUT DRUG TESTING?

Drug testing is something that's talked about a lot, but it's not yet as prevalent as you might think. Even so, don't become complacent: *Random* drug testing *does* occur in Division I football and track and field, for example, on a year-round basis. The testing is mandatory if your team goes to postseason competition—for instance, an NCAA championship tournament or a football bowl game. In the years ahead, drug testing will probably become more common.

What happens if you test positive for drugs? You'll be disqualified from competing for a full season. That's an NCAA regulation. Your college may have its own rules as well regarding your eligibility to play if you've been found using drugs.

Also, as you enter college as a freshman, and then each year thereafter, the NCAA mandates that you sign a drug-testing consent form. If you're participating in a fall sport, this consent form is typically signed when you first report for practice; for sports with seasons beginning later in the academic year, you'll be given the form within four weeks of the start of classes.

To maintain your eligibility—and for many other reasons—I strongly urge you to avoid the use of any illegal substances, whether taken for "recreational" purposes (like cocaine and marijuana) or to enhance your physical strength (like steroids). The NCAA, by the way, also prohibits the use of tobacco products (like chewing tobacco) by athletes during both practices and competition; if you're caught using these products, you will be disqualified from further participation in that particular practice or game.

One other very important point: Living away from home for the first time, you'll be exposed not only to the temptations of drugs but also to alcohol. Every team at every college has a problem with alcohol among some of its players, and it is potential quicksand. Be aware of it and control it.

Imagine yourself walking out of a football stadium after a game in which you and your teammates were cheered by 80,000 screaming fans. (Even if you were on the sidelines, you were part of the hysteria.) The surge of adrenaline will carry over into the evening, and postgame parties are the rule. Yes, there will probably be alcohol and perhaps drugs at these celebrations, but it's crucial not to lose sight of what's at stake. As an eighteen- or nineteen-year-old, you have some tough issues to deal with, and your decisions can affect your future. Be careful.

YOUR ACADEMIC LIFE

Earlier in this book, I have emphasized and reemphasized the importance of academics. No matter how talented you were in high school sports, you wouldn't have gotten into college without your achievements in the classroom, too.

Nothing changes once you get to college. As much as you love to play your sport, and as excited as your college coach is to have you on the team, you won't maintain your eligibility if your commitment to academics falters. Not only will good grades allow you to keep playing but they will put you on the fast track toward getting a college degree. Sports may have helped pave the way for you to get into college, but a college diploma is the ultimate reward.

TAKING ADVANTAGE OF EXTRA ACADEMIC HELP

"Academics have to be a priority in your life, or you're not going to make it in the competitive academic environment of college," says Terri McKeever. "There are a lot of resources at our university to help students be successful, from tutorial services to study groups to counselors who can help you plan your course schedule. But you need to be proactive, and consider your education very important."

As an entering freshman, you'll probably receive some assistance from an academic liaison in the athletic department, helping you select classes and making sure that you're taking enough units to stay eligible. At the same time, you'll begin to meet the lower-division requirements to qualify you for a degree.

Make the most of the study halls that most athletic departments require. If you're having difficulty in a particular class, ask about the availability of tutors to keep you from falling behind. At the college level, you must maintain a C (2.0) average to continue to play, but by taking advantage of extra help when you need it, there is no excuse for backsliding into an academic quagmire.

After four or five years of college, I hope you'll have a scrapbook of athletic memories that will last a lifetime. But in my mind, you haven't made the most of your college experience if you leave school without a diploma. Look at the graduation statistics among athletes at many of the country's finest colleges and you might be shocked to find that only 25, 30, or 40 percent get their degree. Those numbers are a disgrace. (When you were a recruit, you and your parents should have requested or been offered a copy of the Graduation-Rates Report, prepared by the NCAA and pertaining to the Division I or II college interested in you.) Stay motivated, take the college classes you need, and keep up your grades. Develop a relationship with your school counselor or another academic mentor who believes in you and will help bring out your best skills in the classroom, just as your coach does on the playing field. Work with him or her to insure that you're going to graduate. Maybe you'll need an extra semester or two to earn your degree. But make a commitment to stay in college until you get your diploma, whether it takes four, five, or six years.

To help athletes reach this goal, a trend is slowly evolving at some colleges which endows an athlete's scholarship even after his or her sports eligibility is over. At these schools, if an athlete needs an extra semester or an additional year to take the last few remaining classes to graduate, this posteligibility aid will provide the money to help him or her do so—often with the stipulation that the young person participates in a work-study program. Inquire at the athletic department or the financial-aid office of your university about the availability of these funds and ask for an application. As an athlete, you've helped produce revenues for your college; I believe it's only fair for the school to be responsive when you say, "I want to graduate." And NCAA regulations now sanction this additional financial assistance.

So while colleges have traditionally given only lip service to their emphasis on academics for athletes, both parents and their sons and daughters are making it more of an issue. Raise your voice and make sure you get your degree. Remember, a diploma is the most valuable thing you'll take away from your college experience. Yes, perhaps you have dreams of playing sports professionally, but like any other athlete, you're just an injury away from never playing again. So be prepared. Take responsibility for earning your degree. In my mind, student-athletes who graduate should be honored at a banquet much bigger than the one paying tribute to the Heisman Trophy winner.

PLAYING BY THE RULES

A poor academic record is only one factor that can undermine your eligibility to play sports. Another is violating NCAA regulations designed to maintain your amateur status. Not only can you be disqualified from playing by breaching these rules but, depending on the infractions, the college itself could be placed on probation.

Here are important points to keep in mind. The NCAA will consider you a professional, and thus ineligible to play college sports, under the following circumstances:

- You sign a contract, or verbally agree to work with an agent or a professional sports organization.
- You are paid (or are promised payment) to participate in an athletic event or you play on a pro sports team. When playing on an *amateur* sports team, you cannot accept a salary, incentive payment, or expense money (except for a uniform, equipment, actual and necessary travel costs, and room and board).
- You are paid to use your athletic abilities in TV commercials and demonstrations.
- You ask that your name be entered on a professional sports draft list. (There is one exception to this rule: In basketball, you can place your name on a pro draft list *once* and still maintain your college eligibility, as long as you declare your intention in writing to stay in college within thirty days following the draft.)

RESISTING THE TEMPTATIONS

Pro agents have become a serious and ongoing problem at the college level. Talented student-athletes often receive letters and phone calls from agents who offer to represent them down the road in contract talks with pro teams or for appearances in TV commercials. Some come bearing gifts, which can be tempting, particularly for college athletes living on a limited budget.

Even if you have an athletic scholarship, it will cover only the costs of tuition, books, dormitory fees, and meals—it won't give you spending money. To make matters worse, the NCAA prohibits scholarship athletes from holding even a part-time job during the months they're on scholarship. That often leaves college athletes scraping for pocket change, even just to buy gas for their car or to go on a date. Players on a partial scholarship have work-study programs available for them, but those on a full ride face rigid (and I believe unfair) restrictions that prevent them from working except during the summer months.

Nevertheless, resist the temptations that agents may offer. The NCAA does permit you to speak and meet with an agent, but you will be declared ineligible if you sign a contract or make an oral agreement with one, even if the agreement goes into effect only after you leave college. Neither you nor your parents should accept any gifts from agents.

MAKING A COMMITMENT

Your success as a college athlete depends not only on your athletic ability but on the mental toughness you bring with you into the program. As an incoming freshman, create a little tunnel vision, stay focused on your goals, and make a commitment to four to five years of success.

During your college sports career you'll probably experience some rocky periods along the way. For example, you might find yourself as a reserve player, assigned to the second or third unit, and perhaps serving on the scout team during practices. How should you react? Make the best of it and try to impress someone. On the scout team, your job during practices is to play the role of the opponents and help prepare the starters for the next game. At times, you might feel like you've been cast into the outer darkness. But don't shut down. Rather than becoming overwhelmed with frustration by your status, take advantage of the situation. Treat every practice as though it were game day, polish your skills going up against the number-one unit, build a reputation as a go-getter and a dynamo, and force the coaching staff to notice you.

Until you get a chance to play more, stay focused on proving yourself during practices. When I was a college coach, reserve players would sometimes tell me, "I think I should be playing regularly." I'd usually respond, "I couldn't agree with you more; but you need to show me you're ready." I might point out to them the mental errors they were making in practices—perhaps forgetting plays or jumping offside—errors that were undermining their opportunity at a starting job.

TAKE THE INITIATIVE AND PROVE YOURSELF

Brad Muster may have been the best overall player I've ever coached. Brad developed and matured into the Pacific-10 Player of the Year, and the first-round draft selection of the Chicago Bears in 1988. He came into his own at Stanford University, where he impressed our defensive staff, day after day, while he was a member of the scout team; as a result, he was elevated from third string to the starting team—and he never looked back.

I always wanted every one of my athletes to truly believe he was the best player on the team. I wanted them to say, "Coach, I think you're making a mistake in your evaluation of me; I'm going to prove that you're wrong." In fact, you might be the best athlete on the squad—so show it each time you're on the field, whether you're a starter or on the scout team.

Every day, ask yourself questions like, "Do I really want to be excellent? . . . Am I striving to be a champion? . . . Do I want to be the best I can be?" Work hard, but enjoy every minute of your college athletic career, too. Whether your picture is on the front page of the sports section every Saturday, or you spend most of your time on the sidelines or on the bench, your years in college can be among the best in your life—and earn you a college degree in the process. Make the most of this opportunity and relish every minute.

WHEN CIRCUMSTANCES CHANGE

No matter how carefully you choose a college, unexpected events may arise after you arrive at school that affect your status in the athletic program.

For example, coaching changes—involving the head coach or even the entire staff—can happen in any sport and at any college. Competition at your position is also unpredictable, and you may end up with less playing time than you had anticipated. The athletic department at your college might even eliminate your sport completely.

Tim Carey, a talented student-athlete whom I talked about earlier in the book, encountered such unexpected circumstances at Stanford University. After careful deliberation, he decided to transfer to the University of Hawaii, where he was reunited with his former Stanford coach (Fred Von Appen) who had unwavering belief in his talents as a quarterback.

Transferring can be the best situation for all concerned — if it is handled responsibly by both parties. Some colleges, unfortunately, make it difficult for student-athletes to acquire the release necessary to play at another school. Nevertheless, transfers can often be made. I hope that someday the NCAA will allow student-athletes the dignity of choice if a coach is fired or decides to take a job at another university. If a coach can better himself, then why can't a player?

Incidentally, when Tim Carey was contemplating his transfer to the University of Hawaii, he never overlooked the importance of academics. Before his transfer was finalized, he was assured that he could return to Stanford to complete the last quarter of his education, and thus receive a bachelor's degree with the prestigious Stanford name.

IF YOU'RE PLAYING AT A JC

After high school, many young athletes begin their college careers in a junior (or community) college rather than a four-year institution. Sometimes grades are the reason. Or financial considerations may lead them to select a junior college.

Some JC athletes were passed over by most or all four-year-college coaches, who did not consider them to be recruitable players. Maybe they were not perceived as strong enough, fast enough, or talented enough to compete at a four-year college. For such athletes, playing at the junior college level for two years gives them a chance to mature physically and further develop their athletic skills. After two years of JC competition, they may be much more attractive candidates to the same college coaches who had once ignored them. And because JCs are relatively inexpensive, they are a financial bargain for students (and their parents) as they grow athletically, academically, and socially.

MAKING IT TO A FOUR-YEAR COLLEGE

Athletes at the JC level are often motivated by promises that two seasons of competition will get them exposure and a ticket to a four-year college. But that isn't necessarily true. Yes, when major colleges have an immediate need, they often look first for an outstanding JC athlete. After the Division I colleges have picked the top recruits at the JC level, the division II and III colleges select from who's remaining. But, too often, when National Letters of Intent are signed, athletes at two-year colleges are left behind with nowhere to go.

If you're playing at a JC, and particularly in a fall sport like football, I urge you to work hard academically so you can complete your studies there in one-and-a-half years, rather than the traditional two. Carry an extra class each semester. Or take a couple classes in summer school. By doing so, you'll still be able to play two seasons of your sport, get your required academic units, and also be available for spring practice at a four-year college.

KNOW THE RULES

Counselors at your junior college can help make sure you're taking courses that are transferable—although you are ultimately responsible. To make certain you're doing things right, the NCAA provides a free guide ("NCAA Guide for the Two-Year College Student-Athlete") to keep you on track. You need to meet certain requirements to transfer from a JC to a four-year college, and this guide can help insure that you're on course, as well as keep you updated on changes in rules and regulations.

For all JC players, a key is to preserve as much of your eligibility as possible for a four-year college. So become familiar with the regulations that can help you achieve that goal. Some JC athletes, for example, have lost eligibility when they enrolled as full-time students and then decided to drop out—unaware that their NCAA clock kept ticking in that situation. On the other hand, some JC students have enrolled as part-time students (ten units or fewer), and while they may have practiced with the team, they were technically considered "gray shirts" and did not lose any eligibility while getting a jump start on their academic load.

But remember, do not rely on others to do what you need to do yourself. Make sure you know your eligibility status and fully understand how many units you'll need to move on to a four-year college. Every year, hundreds of talented JC athletes become discouraged and disappointed about the recruiting process; do not get caught in the same trap. Take an active role in your academic life. If your grades are not up to par, or you haven't taken the proper, transferable classes, it will eliminate you from the recruiting game quicker than an injury!

LOOKING AHEAD

Going to college, and playing sports at the college level, may be something you've dreamed about for years. I believe this book will help you achieve that goal, and that you'll find college life—academically, athletically, and socially—an enriching and memorable experience.

But in a real sense, making it to college is only a beginning. It is a very important step in helping prepare you for a successful life. Although a college degree and the education it represents provide no guarantees, they will afford you many more options in the years ahead. So rise to the challenge academically, get that degree, and make the most of your college years.

WHAT ABOUT THE PROS?

Like many athletes, you may have hopes of playing your sport professionally. As you enter your junior and senior years, and begin to evaluate how realistic your own pro prospects are, keep in mind that the recruiting process for a pro athlete has similarities to the one you experienced as a high school senior or junior college transfer. Professional teams have regional scouts who are working nearly 365 days a year—talking to college coaches, attending games, watching films, and evaluating talent. By the time the pro draft dates arrive, thousands of hours have been spent by the coaching staffs of these pro teams, defining their needs and narrowing down the lists of players who can help them. It's not a random process; it's as close to a science (albeit an imperfect one) as possible.

If you play college baseball, for example, representatives from major league organizations will probably attend at least some of your games. These scouts may have their eye on a particular athlete whom they consider a top prospect, but even if you're not that player, they'll be watching everyone on the field on both teams, keeping files on what they see—and it's a great opportunity to impress them.

If you play college football, not only are the top prospects being scouted and scrutinized by the pros on Saturday afternoons, but a day will be set aside in the spring in which you and your teammates will be timed in the 40-yard dash by pro representatives. Typically, fifteen to twenty scouts will show up on your practice field, each armed with his own stopwatch, and they'll time everyone on your football team. Each senior's height and weight will also be checked, and you may undergo a skills aptitude test. Based on how well you do, you'll either keep yourself in the chase or find yourself deleted from the prospects list. Those fourteen to eighteen strides from the starting gun to the finish line will help determine your fate as a professional athlete.

While all this is happening, you may be contacted by one or more pro agents, many of whom will be bursting with false promises. You'll hear wild pronouncements like, "Right now, you're probably draftable in the third round but because of my contacts with the pro teams, I can move you up to the first round." Promises like that are bogus. Don't fall prey to those kinds of carrots and put your destiny in someone else's hands. *You* can control your own destiny. Yes, there are people who can assist you, but you need to listen *carefully* to what agents say. Too many of them are concerned only with helping themselves and don't have your interests at heart—but want a hand on your bank account.

WHAT ARE THE ODDS?

More than anything else, if you hope to play in the pros someday, concentrate on proving yourself on the college athletic field. At the same time, however, don't pursue the goal of a professional career at the expense of your other alternatives. Here are some statistics from the NCAA, which indicate just how elite a group the pro athletes are:

- Of the 1 million students who play high school football, only about 150 will make it to the National Football League. The odds of any given high school football player reaching the NFL are about 6,000 to 1.

- Among the 500,000 students who play high school basketball, just 50 will ever play in the National Basketball Association. The chances of any given high school basketball player making it to the NBA are only 10,000 to 1. Fewer than 3 percent of college seniors who play basketball will spend even one year on the roster of an NBA team.

These statistics aren't meant to discourage you. If you have the talent, the drive, and the dream, pursue a pro career as earnestly as you chased the dream of playing in college. But as Cedric W. Dempsey, NCAA executive director, has written, "Take a hard look at those numbers and think about what will matter in the long run—a college education." Whether you play fifteen years in the pros or not a single minute, your college degree will serve you well long after your playing days are over. Studies show that a college diploma produces, on average, a 75 percent increase in earnings over the incomes of those who do *not* earn a degree.

THE REWARDS OF COLLEGE SPORTS

Throughout your athletic life, I think it's important not to lose sight of the big picture. Whether you hope high school and college sports will be a stepping stone to a pro career, or whether you play the game just for the love of it with no expectations of how far you will go, your experiences will be extremely worthwhile and rewarding. You'll learn how to compete, how to function as part of a team, and how to overcome adversity. You'll develop self-discipline and a strong work ethic. And those are qualities and lessons that will be useful in both your personal life and professional career in the future.

Most important, athletics have helped provide you with the opportunity for an education—and not only in the classroom. Most college locker rooms are microcosms of society at large, with young men or women of many races, religions, and national origins. Interacting with these peers will broaden your own horizons and better prepare you for the diverse human experiences you'll continue to encounter in the years ahead.

LIFE AFTER SPORTS

The last portion of my program addresses life after sports. When your playing career is over after high school, college, or the pros, what will you do with the rest of your life? My own proudest accomplishments are found not in the players I've worked with who have made it to the pros but rather in assisting athletes in their next careers, preparing them for life after sports. Fortunately, you'll learn many marketable skills from the sport you play—skills that are valuable to many of America's finest corporations: They include self-direction, the ability to coach and be coached, and the capacity to react and respond to situations in a positive manner. All these skills are transferable to the workplace. Consider the amount of coaching, practicing, refining, and effort that goes into an athletic victory. Think about performing in front of 80,000 people or a national television audience, and making split-second decisions that were the result of countless hours of preparation. Recall how your efforts positively affected your life, as well as the lives of your teammates and coaches.

You are a winner, in the truest sense! Eventually, you can bring what got you here into your next career—the vision, balance, power, flexibility, speed, and heart that guided you every step of the way!

Playing sports at the college level can be a wonderful experience. You've worked hard to get this far, so enjoy it to the fullest—and make sure you graduate, too. Remember, you are an ambassador for our next athletic generation, so give those future players something to live up to—and perhaps surpass! I wish you the best in achieving every one of your goals, now and for the rest of your life.

YOUR COLLEGE-BOUND CHECKLIST

IN THE JUNIOR YEAR . . .

____ Make sure you're on track academically. Take all the core courses you'll need.

____ Fill out and return any questionnaires received from college coaches.

____ Prepare a brief videotape highlighting your athletic skills.

____ Make a list of twenty colleges you'd like to attend.

____ Write letters of introduction to coaches at the twenty schools. Include an unofficial transcript and videotape. Ask about attending a summer camp.

____ About ten days after letters are sent, place calls to coaches.

____ Write to admissions offices of colleges for applications and financial aid information.

IN THE SENIOR YEAR . . .

____ Attend a college sports camp in the summer before your senior year.

____ Make occasional phone calls to college coaches to solidify your relationship.

____ Submit an application for NCAA Initial Eligibility Clearinghouse certification.

____ If coaches visit your home, use the opportunity to get all your questions answered—including the tough ones.

____ Make trips to college campuses.

____ Narrow your college choices. Be sure to submit applications, before the specified deadlines, to the schools you are considering.

____ After each college visit, send a brief follow-up note to the coach.

____ Decide what college to attend. Confirm scholarship and financial aid offers.

____ Sign a National Letter of Intent.

THE NCAA ACADEMIC GUIDELINES: DO YOU MAKE THE GRADE?

The National Collegiate Athletic Association has created academic criteria that student-athletes must meet to compete at the college level (Divisions I and II). Here are the requirements that went into effect in August 1996; they are applicable to students who began college in the 1996–97 academic year:

DIVISION I

These criteria apply to athletes who enter the 305 schools categorized as Division I:

- You must have graduated from high school.
- You must have completed a high school core curriculum of at least thirteen academic courses. These must include the following:

—At least four years of English; at least two years of math (one year each of algebra and geometry, or one year of a higher-level math course for which geometry is a prerequisite).

—At least two years of social sciences; at least two years of natural or physical sciences (including one laboratory class if the high school offers it).

—At least one year of additional courses in math, English, or natural or physical science, and two additional academic courses in any of the previously mentioned areas, or in foreign languages, philosophy, comparative religion, or computer science.

- You must have a grade point average of 2.0 or higher (based on a maximum of 4.0) in your high school core courses, although your GPA may need to be as high as 2.5 depending on your SAT or ACT scores.
- In thirteen courses meeting the core courses criteria listed above, you must have an SAT [Scholastic Aptitude Test] score (combining both the verbal and math sections) that qualifies on the scale below, or

a composite ACT [American College Testing] score (combining the scores on its individual tests) that meets the minimum levels on the same scale.

NCAA ACADEMIC ELIGIBILITY REQUIREMENTS FOR QUALIFIER STATUS

Core GPA	SAT (new scoring system, on or after April 1, 1995)	SAT (old scoring system, before April 1, 1995)	ACT (sum of scores)
2.5 & above	700	700	68
2.475	830	710	69
2.45	840–850	720	70
2.425	860	730	70
2.4	860	740	71
2.375	870	750	72
2.35	880	760	73
2.325	890	770	74
2.3	900	780	75
2.275	910	790	76
2.25	920	800	77
2.225	930	810	78
2.2	940	820	79
2.175	950	830	80
2.15	960	840	80
2.125	960	850	81
2.1	970	860	82
2.075	980	870	83
2.05	990	880	84
2.025	1000	890	85
2.0	1010	900	86

Student-athletes who meet these criteria fit into the category of "qualifier," meaning that as freshmen they can practice and compete and receive an athletic scholarship. However, for those who do not meet these standards, they may be categorized as a "partial qualifier." This status permits them to practice on their college's home field during their freshman year, but they are not permitted to compete during that season. They can receive a college scholarship but are only eligible for three years of competition. Partial qualifiers must graduate from high school, have taken at least thirteen core courses listed earlier, and have the GPA scores and the corresponding SAT/ACT minimum qualifications in the box below.

NCAA ACADEMIC ELIGIBILITY REQUIREMENTS FOR PARTIAL QUALIFIER STATUS

Core GPA	SAT (new scoring system)	SAT (old scoring system)	ACT (sum of scores)
2.75 & above	720	600	59
2.725	730	610	59
2.7	730	620	60
2.675	740–750	630	61
2.65	760	640	62
2.625	770	650	63
2.6	780	660	64
2.575	790	670	65
2.55	800	680	66
2.525	810	690	67

These academic requirements have actually been tightened in the past few years. In fact, as recently as the 1994–95 academic year, guidelines known as Proposition 48 required a QUALIFIER minimum combined score of 700 on the verbal and math components of the SAT (old scoring system). But as the new table indicates, if you have a 2.0 GPA, you need a much higher SAT score (900 in the old system) for athletic eligibility. With a 2.25 GPA, you'll need 800 on the SATs (old scoring system). So the higher your GPA, the less pressure you'll feel when taking the SATs—another good reason to work hard to excel in the classroom.

DIVISION II

If you're considering attending a Division II college, the academic criteria for student-athletes are not exactly the same as with Division I

schools. Here are the changes that apply to Division II to attain qualifier status, and thus enable you to practice and compete as a freshman
and receive an athletic scholarship:

- Although you still need to take thirteen core academic courses in
  high school, these classes must include three (rather than four)
  English courses.

- You need one (not two) years of additional courses in English,
  math, or natural or physical science.

- While there is no table for Division II providing minimum corresponding scores of Core GPA and SAT/ACT scores, you must
  have achieved the following:

—A GPA of 2.0 in at least 13 core academic courses.

—A minimum SAT score of 820 (new scoring system) or 700 (old
scoring system); or a minimum ACT score of 68 (sum of scores on the
individual tests).

THE NATIONAL LETTER OF INTENT

The following is a copy of the 1997 National Letter of Intent from the Collegiate Commissioners Association. Note that this is a sample and isn't intended for official use. To find out more about the National Letter of Intent, write to the CAA, c/o Southeastern Conference, 2201 Civic Center Blvd., Birmingham, AL 35203.

1997 NATIONAL LETTER OF INTENT (NLI)
ADMINISTERED BY THE COLLEGIATE COMMISSIONERS ASSO-
CIATION (CCA)

Do not sign prior to 7:00 am (local time) on the following dates
or after the final signing date listed for each sport.

SPORT	INITIAL SIGNING DATE	FINAL SIGNING DATE
_____ Basketball (Early Period)	November 13, 1996	November 20, 1996
_____ Basketball (Late Period)	April 9, 1997	May 15, 1997
_____ Football (Midyear JC Transfer)	December 18, 1996	January 15, 1997
_____ Football (Regular Period)	February 5, 1997	April 1, 1997
_____ W Volleyball, Field Hockey, Soccer, M Water Polo	February 5, 1997	August 1, 1997
_____ All Other Sports (Early Period)	November 13, 1996	November 20, 1996
_____ All Other Sports (Late Period)	April 9, 1997	August 1, 1997

(Place an "X" on the proper line)

173

IMPORTANT—READ CAREFULLY

It is important to read this entire document before signing it in triplicate. One copy is to be retained by you and two copies are to be returned to the institution, one of which will be filed with the appropriate conference commissioner.

---

1. **Initial Enrollment in Four-Year Institution.** This NLI is applicable only to prospective student-athletes who will be entering four-year institutions for the first time as full-time students, except for 4-2-4 transfers who are graduating from junior college as outlined in paragraph 8-b.

2. **Financial Aid Requirement.** I must receive in writing an award for athletics financial aid for the entire 1997–98 academic year from the institution named in this document at the time of my signing. A mid-year junior college transfer must receive athletics financial aid for the remainder of the 1996–97 academic year. The award letter shall list the terms and conditions of the award, including the amount and duration of the financial aid. If such conditions are not met, this NLI shall be declared null and void, <u>and the institution which submits such a letter shall be in violation of the NLI Program and may be subject to appropriate sanctions.</u>

   a. **Professional Sports Contract.** If I sign a professional sports contract, I will remain bound by the provisions of this NLI even if the institution named in this document is prohibited from making athletically-related financial aid available to me under NCAA rules.

3. **Provisions of Letter Satisfied.**

   a. **One-year Attendance Requirement Met.** The terms of this NLI shall be satisfied if I attend the institution named in this document for at least one academic year.

   b. **Junior College Graduation.** The terms of this NLI shall be satisfied if I graduate from junior college after signing a NLI while in high school or during my first year in junior college.

4. **Basic Penalty.** I understand that if I do not attend the institution named within this document for one full academic year, and I enroll in another institution participating in the NLI program, I may not represent the latter institution in intercollegiate athletics competition until I have completed two full academic years of residence at the latter institution. Further, I understand that I shall be charged with the loss of two seasons of intercollegiate athletics competition in all sports, except as otherwise provided in this NLI. This is in addition to any eligibility expended at the institution at which I initially enrolled.

a. Early Signing Period Penalties. A prospective student-athlete who signs a NLI during the early signing period (November 13–20, 1996) will be ineligible for practice and competition in football for a two-year period and also shall be charged with two seasons of competition in the sport of football.

5. **Mutual Release Agreement.** A formal release procedure shall be provided in the event the institution and I mutually agree to release each other from any obligations to the NLI. I understand that if I receive this formal release, I shall not be eligible for competition at a second NLI institution during my first academic year of residence there, and I shall lose one season of competition. This mutual release form must be signed by me, my parent or legal guardian, and the Director of Athletics of the institution named in this document, and I must file a copy of the mutual release form with the conference which processes this NLI. (NOTE: this mutual release form may be obtained from the institution named in this document.)

a. Authority to Release. A coach is not authorized to void, cancel or give a release to this NLI.

b. Extent of Mutual Release. A mutual release from this NLI shall apply to all participating institutions and shall not be conditional or selective by institution.

6. **Appeal Process.** I understand that the NLI Steering Committee has been authorized to issue interpretations, settle disputes and consider petition for a full release from the provisions of this NLI where there are extenuating circumstances. I further understand its decision may be appealed to the NLI Appeals Committee, whose decision shall be final and binding.

7. **Letter Becomes Null and Void.** This NLI shall be declared null and void if any of the following occurs:

a. Admissions Requirement. This NLI shall be declared null and void if the institution with which I signed notifies me in writing that I have been denied admission.

(1) It is presumed that I am eligible for admission and financial aid until information is submitted to the contrary. Thus, it is mandatory for me, upon request, to provide a transcript of my previous academic record and an application for admission to the institution named in this document.

(2) If I am eligible for admission, but the institution named in this document defers admission to a subsequent term, this NLI shall be rendered null and void. However, if I defer my admission, the NLI remains binding.

b. Eligibility Requirements. This NLI shall be declared null and void if, by the institution's opening day of classes in the fall of 1997, I have not met (a) the institution's requirements for admission, (b) its academic requirements for financial aid to athletes, **AND** (c) the NCAA requirement for freshman financial aid (NCAA Bylaw 14.3) or the NCAA junior college transfer rule.

(1) If I become a nonqualifier (per NCAA Bylaw 14.3), this NLI shall be rendered null and void.

(2) If I am midyear junior college football transfer signee, the NLI remains binding for the following fall term if I was eligible for admission and financial aid and met the junior college transfer requirements for competition for the winter or spring term, but chose to delay my admission.

c. One-Year Absence. This NLI shall be null and void if I have not attended any institution (or attended an institution, including a junior college, that does not participate in the NLI Program) for at least one academic year after signing this NLI, provided my request for athletics financial aid for a subsequent fall term is not approved by the institution with which I signed. To receive this waiver, I must file with the appropriate conference commissioner a statement from the Director of Athletics at the institution named in this document that such finanial aid will not be available to me for the requested fall term.

d. Service in the U.S. Armed Forces. Church Mission. This NLI shall be null and void if I serve on active duty with the armed forces of the United States or an official church mission for at least eighteen (18) months.

e. Discontinued Sport. This NLI shall be null and void if my sport is discontinued by the institution named in the document.

f. Recruiting Rules Violation. If the institution (or a representative of its athletics interests) named in this document violated NCAA or conference rules while recruiting me, as found through the NCAA or conference enforcement process or acknowledged by the institution, this NLI shall be declared null and void. Such declaration shall not take place until all appeals to the NCAA or conference for restoration of eligibility have been concluded.

8. **Only One Valid NLI Permitted.** I understand that I may sign only one valid NLI, except as listed below.

a. **Subsequent Signing Year.** If this NLI is rendered null and void under Item 7, I remain free to enroll in any institution of my choice where I am admissible and shall be permitted to sign another NLI in a subsequent signing year.

b. Junior College Exception. If I signed a NLI while in high school or during my first year in junior college, I may sign another NLI in the signing year in which I am scheduled to graduate from junior college. If I graduate, the second NLI shall be binding on me; otherwise, the original NLI I signed shall remain valid.

9. **Recruiting Ban After Signing.** I understand that all participating conferences and institutions are obligated to respect my signing and shall cease to recruit me upon my signing this NLI. I shall notify any recruiter who contacts me that I have signed.

10. **Institutional Signatures Required Prior to Submission.** This NLI must be signed and dated by the Director of Athletics or his/her authorized representative before submission to me and my parents (or legal guardian) for our signatures. This NLI may be mailed prior to the initial signing date. When a NLI is issued prior to the initial signing date, the "date of issuance" shall be considered to be the initial signing date and not the date that the NLI was signed or mailed by the institution.

11. **Parent/Guardian Signature Required.** My parent or legal guardian is required to sign this NLI if I am less than 21 years of age at the time of my signing, regardless of my marital status. If I do not have a living parent or a legal guardian, this NLI may be signed by the person who is acting in the capacity of a guardian. An explanation of the circumstances shall accompany this NLI.

12. **Falsification of NLI.** If I falsify any part of this NLI, or if I have knowledge that my parent or guardian falsified any part of this NLI, I understand that I shall forfeit the first two years of my eligibility at any NLI participating institution as outlined in Item 4.

13. **14-Day Signing Deadline.** If my parent or legal guardian and I fail to sign this NLI within **14 days** of issuance to me, it will be invalid. In that event, another NLI may be issued within the appropriate signing period. (**NOTE**: This does not apply to the early signing period.)

14. **Institutional Filing Deadline.** This NLI must be filed with the appropriate conference by the institution named in this document within 21 days after the date of final signature or it will be invalid. In that event, another NLI may be issued.

15. **No Additions or Deletions Allowed to NLI.** No additions or deletions may be made to this NLI or the Mutual Release Agreement.

16. Official Time for Validity. This NLI shall be considered to be officially signed on the final date of signature by myself or my parent (or guardian). If no time of day is listed, then 11:59 p.m. is presumed.

17. Statute of Limitations. This NLI shall carry a four-year statute of limitations.

18. Nullification of Other Agreements. My signature on this NLI nullifies any agreements, oral or otherwise, which would release me from the conditions stated within this NLI.

> **19. If Coach Leaves.** I understand that I have signed this NLI with the institution and not for a particular sport or individual. For example, if the coach leaves the institution or the sports program, I remain bound by the provisions of the NLI.

20. Coaching Contact Prohibited at Time of Signing. <u>A coach or an institutional representative may not hand-deliver this NLI off campus or be present off campus at the time I sign it.</u> This NLI may be delivered by express mail, courier service, regular mail or facsimile machine.

COLLEGIATE COMMISSIONERS ASSOCIATION

NATIONAL LETTER OF INTENT PROGRAM

1997 National Letter of Intent (NLI)

Name of Prospect _____
                Last   First   Middle
       (Type Proper Name, Including Middle Name or Initial)

Permanent Address _____
           Street   City   State   Zip Code

Sumission of this NLI has been authorized by:

SIGNED _____   _____
        Director of Athletics   Date Issued to Prospect

_____   _____
    Sport (Men's)   Sport (Women's)

☐ Check here if signee is a junior college transfer student.

This is to certify my decision to enroll at_____
                       Name of Institution

I certify that I have read all terms and conditions included in the four pages of this document. I have discussed them with the coach and/or other staff representatives of the institution named above, and I fully understand, accept and agree to be bound by them. *(All three copies of this NLI must be signed individually.)*

SIGNED _____ _____ _____
    Prospect's Signature   Date (Mth/Day/Yr) Time (A.M./P.M.)

_____
Prospect's Social Security Number

SIGNED _____ _____ _____
    Parent or Legal Guardian   Date (Mth/Day/Yr) Time (A.M./P.M.)
    Signature (circle one)
(required if student-athlete has not reached 21st birthday)

_____ _____
Print Name of Parent/Legal Guardian   Telephone Number
                            (including area code)

COLLEGE CONTACTS: ADDRESSES AND PHONE NUMBERS

As part of you own campaign to gain the attention of college coaches in your sport, I suggest that you make phone calls and send letters to coaches at twenty colleges that you'd like to attend (see chapter 6). The following list is only a sampling of America's colleges (with mailing addresses and athletic-department phone numbers), but it will give you an idea of the types of schools classified as Divisions I, II, and III by the National Collegiate Athletic Association. For a complete list of colleges, see the reference books available in your high school counseling center or at the public library.

DIVISION I

Appalachian State University
Owens Fieldhouse
Boone, NC 28608
(704) 262–4010

Arizona State University
Box 872505
Tempe, AZ 85287–2505
(602) 965–3636

Auburn University
P.O. Box 351
Auburn, AL 36831–0351
(205) 844–4750

Ball State University
2000 University Ave.
Muncie, IN 47306
(317) 258–8225

Baylor University
3031 Dutton
Waco, TX 76711
(817) 755–1234

Boston University
285 Babcock St.
Boston, MA 02215
(617) 353–4630

Bowling Green State University
Bowling Green, OH 43403
(419) 372–2401

Brigham Young University
P.O. Box 22240
106 Smith Fieldhouse
Provo, UT 84602–2240
(801) 378–2096

Brown University
Hope St.
Providence, RI 02912
(401) 863–2211

California State University
(Fullerton)
P.O. Box 34080
Fullerton, CA 92634–9480
(714) 773–3058

California State University
(Sacramento)
6000 J St.
Sacramento, CA 95819–6099
(916) 278–6481

Central Michigan University
Rose Center
Mt. Pleasant, MI 48859
(517) 774–3041

Chicago State University
95th & King Dr.
Chicago, IL 60628
(312) 995–2295

Clemson University
Box 31, 1 Perimeter Rd.
Clemson, SC 29633
(803) 656–2101

Colorado State University
Fort Collins, CO 80523
(303) 491–5300

Columbia University
Dodge Physical Fitness Center
New York, NY 10027
(212) 854–2538

Dartmouth College
6083 Alumni Gym
Hanover, NH 03755–3512
(603) 646–2465

Duke University
Cameron Indoor Stadium
Durham, NC 27708
(919) 684–2120

East Central University
E. 14th St.
Ada, OK 74820
(405) 436–8000

East Tennessee State University
Walnut & University Parkway
Johnson City, TN 37614
(615) 929–4343

Eastern Illinois University
Lantz Building, Grant St.
Charleston, IL 61920
(217) 581–2319

Eastern Michigan University
Bowen Fieldhouse
Ypsilanti, MI 48197
(313) 487–1849

Florida State University
P.O. Box 2195
Tallahassee, FL 32316
(904) 644–1079

Fresno State University
5305 N. Campus Dr.
Fresno, CA 93740–0027
(209) 278–2643

George Washington University
600 22nd St., N.W.
Washington, D.C. 20052
(202) 994–6650

Georgetown University
3700 O St., N.W.
Washington, D.C. 20057–1956
(202) 687–2435

Georgia Tech
150 Bobby Dodd Way, N.W.
Atlanta, GA 30332–0445
(404) 894–5400

Gonzaga University
E. 502 Boone Ave.
Spokane, WA 99258
(509) 328–4220, ext. 4203

Grambling State University
Box 868
Grambling, LA 71245
(318) 274–2634

Harvard University
60 John F. Kennedy St.
Cambridge, MA 02138
(617) 495–2204

Howard University
6th & Girard Sts., N.W.
Washington, D.C. 20059
(202) 806–7140

Idaho State University
Box 8173, Holt Arena
Pocatello, ID 83209
(208) 236–2771

Illinois State University
2660 Redbird Arena #213
Normal, IL 61790–2660
(309) 438–3633

Indiana State University
Terre Haute, IN 47809
(812) 237–4040

Indiana University
Athletic Dept., Assembly Hall
Bollmington, IN 47405
(812) 855–2794

Iowa State University
1800 S. 4th St.
Ames, IA 50011
(515) 294–3662

Jackson State University
1325 W. Lynch St.
Jackson, MS 39217
(601) 968–2291

James Madison University
S. Main St.
Harrisonburg, VA 22807
(703) 568–6164

Kansas State University
1800 College Ave.
Manhattan, KS 66502–3355
(913) 532–6910

Kent State University
Kent, OH 44242
(216) 672–5976

Long Beach State University
1250 Bellflower Blvd.
Long Beach, CA 90840
(310) 985–4655

Long Island University
　(Brooklyn Center)
University Plaza
Brooklyn, NY 11201
(718) 488–1030

Louisiana State University
P.O. Box 25095
Baton Rouge, LA 70894–5095
(504) 388–6606

Loyola Marymount University
7101 W. 80th St.
Los Angeles, CA 90046
(213) 338–2765

Manhattan College
Manhattan College Parkway
Riverdale, NY 10471
(718) 920–0227

Marquette University
1212 W. Wisconsin Ave.
Milwaukee, WI 53233
(412) 288–6303

Miami University
Millett Hall
Oxford, OH 45056
(513) 529–3113

Michigan State University
213 Jenison Field House
East Lansing, MI 48824
(517) 355–9710

Mississippi State University
P.O. Drawer 5327
Mississippi State, MS 39762
(601) 325–2532

Montana State University
#1 Bobcat Circle
Bozeman, MT 59717–0338
(406) 994–0211

Morehouse College
Atlanta, GA 30314
(404) 215–2669

New Mexico State University
Box 3145
Las Cruces, NM 88003
(505) 646–4126

Northern Illinois University
DeKalb, IL 60115
(815) 753–1295

Northwestern University
1501 Central St.
Evanston, IL 60208–3630
(708) 491–3205

Ohio State University
410 Woody Hayes Dr.
Columbus, OH 43210
(614) 292–7572

Oklahoma State University
Stillwater, OK 74078–0300
(405) 744–7740

Oregon State University
Gill Coliseum
Corvallis, OR 97331–4105
(503) 737–2547

Pennsylvania State University
(University Park)
University Park, PA 16802
(814) 863–1000

Pepperdine University
24255 Pacific Coast Highway
Malibu, CA 90263
(310) 456–4150

Princeton University
P.O. Box 71
Jadwin Gym
Princeton, NJ 08544
(609) 258–3534

Purdue University
W. Lafayette, IN 47907
(317) 494–3189

Rice University
P.O. Box 1892
Houston, TX 77251
(713) 527–4077

San Diego State University
San Diego, CA 92182
(619) 549–5163

San Jose State University
One Washington Square
San Jose, CA 95192–0062
(408) 924–1200

Southern Methodist University
6024 Airline Rd.
Box 750216
Dallas, TX 75275–0216
(214) 768–2864

Stanford University
Stanford, CA 94305
(415) 723–4591

Syracuse University
Manley Field House
Syracuse, NY 13244–5020
(315) 443–2385

Temple University
McGonigle Hall
Philadelphia, PA 19122
(215) 204–7447

Texas A & M University
College Station, TX 77843–1228
(409) 845–1241

United States Air Force Academy
2169 Cadet Fieldhouse Dr.,
   Suite 100
Air Force Academy, CO
   80840–9500
(719) 472–4008

United States Military Academy
   (Army)
West Point, NY 10996
(914) 938–2973

United States Naval Academy
   (Navy)
Annapolis, MD 21402
(410) 293–6220

University of Akron
Akron, OH 44325-5201
(216) 972–7080

University of Alabama
   (Birmingham)
617 13th St.
Birmingham, AL 35294–1160
(205) 934–4011

University of Arizona
McKale Center
Tucson, AZ 85721
(602) 621–2200

University of Arkansas
   (Fayetteville)
Broyles Athletic Complex
Fayetteville, AR 72701
(501) 575–6533

University of California
   (Berkeley)
Berkeley, CA 94720
(510) 642–0580

University of California (Irvine)
Irvine, CA 92717
(714) 856–6931

University of California
   (Los Angeles) /U.C.L.A.
405 Hilgard Ave.
Los Angeles, CA 90024
(310) 825–8699

University of Cincinnati
Cincinnati, OH 45221–0021
(513) 556–5601

University of Colorado
Campus Box 368
Boulder, CO 80309
(303) 492–7931

University of Connecticut
2095 Hillside Rd.
Storrs, CT 06269–3078
(203) 486–2725

University of Delaware
Bob Carpenter Center
S. College Ave.
Newark, DE 19716
(302) 831–4006

University of Florida
Box 14485
Gainesville, FL 32604
(904) 375–4683

University of Georgia
P.O. Box 1472
Athens, GA 30613
(706) 542–1306

University of Hawaii (Manoa)
1337 Lower Campus Rd.
Honolulu, HI 96822–2370
(808) 956–7301

University of Houston
Houston, TX 77204–5121
(713) 743–9370

University of Idaho
Kibbie-ASUI Activity Center
Moscow, ID 83844–2302
(208) 885–0200

University of Illinois (Chicago)
901 W. Roosevelt Rd.
Chicago, IL 60608
(312) 996–2772

University of Illinois (Urbana-
    Champaign)
1817 S. Neil St., Suite 201
Champaign, IL 61820
(217) 333–3631

University of Iowa
Iowa City, IA 52242
(319) 335–9327

University of Kansas
Allen Fieldhouse
Lawrence, KS 66045–8881
(913) 864–3143

University of Kentucky
Memorial Coliseum
Lexington, KY 40506–0019
(606) 257–8000

University of Louisville
Louisville, KY 40292
(502) 852–5732

University of Maine
5747 Memorial Gym
Orono, ME 04469–5747
(207) 581–1058

University of Maryland
P.O. Box 295
College Park, MD 20741–0295
(301) 314–7075

University of Massachusetts
    (Amherst)
Boyden Bldg.
Amherst, MA 01003
(413) 545–2342

University of Memphis
470 Normal
Memphis, TN 38152
(901) 678–2331

University of Miami
#1 Hurricane Dr.
Coral Gables, FL 33146
(305) 284–3822

University of Michigan
1000 S. State St.
Ann Arbor, MI 48109
(313) 747–2583

University of Minnesota
(Twin Cities)
516 15th Ave., S.E.
Minneapolis, MN 55455
(612) 625–4838

University of Mississippi
University, MS 38677
(601) 232–7241

University of Missouri
P.O. Box 677
Hearnes Center
Columbia, MO 65205
(573) 882–6501

University of Montana
Missoula, MT 59812
(406) 243–5331

University of Nebraska (Lincoln)
103 S. Stadium
Lincoln, NE 68588–0120
(402) 472–4224

University of Nevada (Reno)
Lawlor Annex, Mailstop 232
Reno, NV 89557
(702) 784–6900

University of Nevada (Las
Vegas)/U.N.L.V.
4505 Maryland Parkway
Las Vegas, NV 89154
(702) 895–3614

University of New Mexico
South Campus
Albuquerque, NM 87131
(505) 277–0111

University of North Carolina
Chapel Hill, NC 27514
(919) 962–6000

University of Notre Dame
Notre Dame, IN 46556
(219) 631–7456

University of Oklahoma
180 W. Brooks
Room 201
Norman, OK 73019
(405) 325–8200

University of Oregon
2727 Leo Harris Parkway
Eugene, OR 97401
(503) 346–4481

University of Pennsylvania
Weightman Hall N.
Philadelphia, PA 19104–6322
(215) 898–6121

University of Pittsburgh
P.O. Box 7436
Pittsburgh, PA 15213
(412) 648–8200

University of South Carolina
Columbia, SC 29208
(803) 777–4202

University of Southern California
University Park
Los Angeles, CA 90089–0602
(213) 740–3843

University of Tennessee
1720 Volunteer Blvd.
Knoxville, TN 37996–3100
(615) 974–1212

University of Texas (Austin)
P.O. Box 7399
Austin, TX 78713–7399
(512) 471–4602

University of Utah
Jon M. Huntsman Center
Salt Lake City, UT 84112
(801) 581–8171

University of Vermont
Patrick Gym
Burlington, VT 05405
(802) 656–3074

University of Virginia
P.O. Box 3785
University Hall
Charlottesville, VA 22903
(804) 982–5000

University of Washington
Graves Building
Seattle, WA 98195
(206) 543–2210

University of Wisconsin
  (Madison)
1440 Monroe St.
Madison, WI 53771
(608) 262–1866

Utah State University
UMC 7400
Logan, UT 84322–7400
(801) 797–1850

Vanderbilt University
Box 120158
2601 Jess Neely Dr.
Nashville, TN 37212
(615) 322–4727

Villanova University
Villanova, PA 19085
(610) 519–4130

Washington State University
107 Bohler Gym
Pullman, WA 99164–1610
(509) 335–0311

West Virginia University
Box 0877
Morgantown, WV 26507–0877
(304) 293–5621

Wichita State University
Campus Box 18
1845 Fairmount
Wichita, KS 67260–0018
(316) 689–3250

Yale University
Ray Tompkins House
20 Tower Parkway
P.O. Box 208216
New Haven, CT 06520–8216
(203) 432–4747

DIVISION II

Albany State College
504 College Dr.
Albany, GA 31705
(912) 430–4754

Barry University
11300 N.E. 2nd Ave.
Miami Shores, FL 33161
(305) 899–3550

Bloomsburg University
Bloomsburg, PA 17815
(717) 389–4050

Brandeis University
415 South St.
Waltham, MA 02254–9110
(617) 736–3661

California Polytechnic State
   University
1 Grand Ave.
San Luis Obispo, CA 93407
(805) 756–2923

City College of New York
138th St. & Convent Ave.
New York, NY 10031
(212) 650–8228

Columbus College
4225 University Ave.
Columbus, GA 31907–5645
(706) 568–2204

Delta State University
Box A-3
Cleveland, MS 38733
(601) 846–4300

East Texas State University
E. Texas Station
Commerce, TX 75429
(903) 886–5549

Hampton University
Hampton, VA 23668
(804) 727–5641

Humboldt State University
Arcata, CA 95521
(707) 826–5446

Jacksonville State University
700 Pelham Rd. N.
Jacksonville, AL 36265–9982
(205) 782–5365

Mansfield University
Academy St.
Mansfield, PA 16933
(717) 662–4860

Millersville University
N. George St.
Millersville, PA 17551
(717) 872–3361

Mississippi College
P.O. Box 4245
Clinton, MS 39058
(601) 925–3341

Missouri Valley College
500 E. College
Marshall, MO 65340
(816) 886–6924

Norfolk State University
2401 Corprew Ave.
Norfolk, VA 23504
(804) 683–8600

Northern Michigan University
Presque Isle Ave.
Marquette, MI 49855–5349
(906) 227–2105

Portland State University
P.O. Box 751
Portland, OR 97207
(503) 725–4000

Queens College
Kissena Blvd.
Flushing, NY 11367
(718) 520–7215

University of California (Davis)
Davis, CA 95616
(916) 752–1111

University of California
   (Riverside)
Riverside, CA 92521
(909) 787–5432

University of Central Arkansas
Donaghey & Bruce St.
Conway, AR 72035–0001
(501) 450–3150

University of New Haven
300 Orange Ave.
West Haven CT 06516
(203) 932–7017

University of North Dakota
Grand Forks, ND 58202
(701) 777–2234

University of South Dakota
414 E. Clark St.
Vermillion, SD 57069–2390
(605) 677–5309

DIVISION III

Allegheny College
P.O. Box 34
Meadville, PA 16335
(814) 332–3367

Binghamton University (SUNY)
P.O. Box 6000
Binghamton, NY 13902–6000
(607) 777–4255

Buffalo State College
1300 Elmwood Ave.
Buffalo, NY 14222
(716) 878–4000

Catholic University of America
620 Michigan Ave., N.E.
Washington, DC 20064
(202) 319–5287

Elmhurst College
190 Prospect
Elmhurst, IL 60126
(708) 617–3140

Emory University
Woodruff PE Center
600 Asbury Circle
Atlanta, GA 30322
(404) 727–6547

Fitchburg State College
Pearl St.
Fitchburg, MA 01420
(617) 345–2151 (ext. 3314)

Framingham State College
100 State St.
Framingham, MA 01701
(508) 626–4614

Gettysburg College
Box 400
Gettysburg, PA 17325
(717) 337–6400

Hunter College (CUNY)
695 Park Ave.
New York, NY 10021
(212) 772–4783

Ithaca College
Ceracche Athletic Center
Ithaca, NY 14850–7198
(607) 274–3209

Jersey City State College
2039 Kennedy Blvd.
Jersey City, NJ 07305
(201) 200–3317

Johns Hopkins University
Charles & 34th Sts.
Baltimore, MD 21218
(410) 516–7490

Massachusetts Institute of
    Technology
P.O. Box D
Cambridge, MA 02139–4307
(617) 253–4498

Montclair State University
Upper Montclair, NJ 07043
(201) 655–5234

New York University
Washington Square
181 Mercer St.
New York, NY 10012
(212) 998–2030

Rutgers (State University of
    New Jersey)
P.O. Box 5061
Gymnasium College Ave.
New Brunswick, NJ 08903–5061
(908) 932–8610

State University of New York
  (Stony Brook)
Nicholls Road
Stony Brook, NY 11794–3500
(516) 632–7205

University of Chicago
5640 S. University Ave.
Chicago, IL 60637
(312) 702–7681

University of Redlands
P.O. Box 3080
1200 E. Colton Ave.
Redlands, CA 92373–0999
(909) 335–4004

University of Rochester
Alumni Gymnasium
Rochester, NY 14627–0296
(716) 275–4301

ABOUT THE AUTHORS

Jim Walsh

Jim Walsh knows the world of college sports recruiting inside and out. As a high school student he was a four-sport letterman, courted to play football by the likes of Notre Dame and USC. An injury in his senior year dampened the interest of the "marquee" colleges, but Jim bounced back to become a star running back for San Jose State and went on to play professionally with the Seattle Seahawks.

Following his pro career, Jim became an assistant coach and recruiter for Stanford University and San Jose State, positions that brought him in contact with literally thousands of high school student-athletes. In 1988, he left the coaching field to start A STEP BEYOND, a consulting program through which he helps students fulfill their potential and achieve their goal of playing college sports. Jim has worked with over 5,000 clients and has successfully placed 100 percent of them in college sports programs. Five of Jim's clients have gone on to be first-round professional draft picks, and numerous others have become pro signees.

Richard Trubo

Richard Trubo is the author or coauthor of more than a dozen books, including several in the fields of self-help and sports. He cowrote *Secrets of Soviet Sports Fitness and Training*, and has written for many magazines and newspapers, including the *New York Times, Los Angeles Times, Chicago Tribune, American Health, Reader's Digest,* and *Parade*. He has received several journalism awards for excellence in writing.